THE GUTS TO WIN

JANE BLALOCK

With Dwayne Netland
Introduction by BILLIE JEAN KING

A Golf Digest Book

Published by Golf Digest, Inc. **NYT**
A New York Times Company
495 Westport Avenue
Norwalk, Connecticut 06856

Trade book distribution by
Simon and Schuster
1230 Avenue of the Americas
New York, New York 10020

First printing
ISBN: 0–914178–12–1
Library of Congress: 77–073011
Manufactured in the United States
of America

ACKNOWLEDGEMENTS

Golf has become such a dominant influence in my life that I feel compelled to share with the readers of this book much of what I have learned and experienced. The theme throughout is the wonderful appeal of competition, of striving for a goal, that is now possible for women in so many different areas of sport.

I hope that by relating some of the incidents of my own playing career I will contribute to a deeper understanding and appreciation of golf for the many thousands of women who play the game on both social and competitive levels.

No description of my involvement with golf would be complete without an intensive review of my conflict with the LPGA resulting from the cheating charges and the lawsuit of 1972. The repercussions were so widespread that I have devoted two chapters to the episode, although I have attempted to keep them in perspective with the overall topic of competitiveness.

One of the most unfortunate aspects about the ordeal I endured is that it concluded without a winner, financially or emotionally. Regardless of the number of tournaments I may win or the number of awards I may receive, will the sporting public ever really believe that I was innocent?

I often talk about the incident being forgotten, but the cold truth is that I will never be totally vindicated in my time. Part of my purpose in writing the book is to fulfill a desire that I have had since the day I was suspended. Perhaps it is a release of frustration and a biting desire to tell my side of the story, something the courts forbade until the case was settled.

I must thank my family, who provided me with the opportunity to pursue the game I love and, when that opportunity was nearly taken from me, gave me endless support. I shall never forget my friends who remained loyal. I don't have to name them here, because they know who they are.

Acknowledgment should also be made to the new LPGA, which has erased the past and brought the women's tour to unprecedented prosperity. I'm pleased to be part of this growing organization, not only for the financial and competitive opportunities it affords, but because of the inspiration it provides the young women of today who will progress in the years ahead and make their mark on the tour.

I'm grateful to *Golf Digest* for publishing the book and to the many members of its staff who played important roles—Associate Publisher Paul Menneg, who encouraged me to pursue the project; Ross Goodner, Charlene Cruson, Bill Jarrett and Nick Seitz, who all had a hand in editing the text; Laura Duggan for her attractive book design and

Lois Jamieson for her efforts in typing the manuscript and rounding up many of the photos.

Special thanks go to my collaborator, Dwayne Netland of *Golf Digest*. We spent countless hours together in the research and preparation of the manuscript. I know he feels that the grind of digging through court documents, checking and re-checking facts and sitting through our long taping sessions was compensated by our lighter moments on the golf course, on plane flights and in restaurants. I think we made a good team.

—Jane Blalock
Highland Beach, Fla.
February, 1977

INTRODUCTION

I suppose it was inevitable that two professional athletes with such similar temperaments and outlooks as Janie Blalock and myself should eventually be drawn together, partially out of admiration for the other's skills in her sport and partially out of a common competitive bond.

The fact that each of us has also fought for the betterment of women's sports in general was undoubtedly another factor in the formation of our friendship. I was delighted to read in her book that Janie has touched upon the growing opportunities for women in many areas of sport.

Few people I know are better qualified to discuss the alluring appeal of competition, because Janie is first and foremost a competitor, one of the toughest and most determined I have ever met. Considering what she has had to endure, the quality has been a priceless asset in her struggle to the top.

I have some understanding of what Janie went through in her long and bitter legal squabble with the LPGA, since I faced the hostility of fellow competitors myself in another arena. In 1968 Ann Jones, Françoise Durr, Rosemary Casals and myself turned professional with the National Tennis League. The decision resulted not just from the money, but for the chance to tell the world, "Yes, I am a professional." None of us realized how our newly proclaimed status would change us in the eyes of our fellow tennis players. The simple fact we had declared ourselves professionals and signed guaranteed contracts made us pariahs in their minds. We were shunned, cold-shouldered and made to feel out of the group.

In retrospect, that was nothing compared to what Janie went through in golf. There were four of us. She stood alone. We were considered guilty of being different because we were honest enough to stand up to the hypocrisy of amateur tennis. Janie was accused by her peers without a trial. I cannot think of a more lonely place to be.

At the time Janie's problems began, I had known her for only a short while. I was impressed with her skill and her drive. A lesser person might have crumbled under that type of pressure. Janie improved her game, and came into her own as both a golfer and a person.

In the process, she displayed another admirable characteristic. Most athletes are takers. They will give time and advice to youngsters on the way up, but rarely will they invest financially in the futures of others. Janie and I founded the Connecticut Falcons of Women's Professional Softball. For her, it was a reflection of a unique facet of a unique personality.

The softball league will be a challenge for all of us involved, but I don't have to tell you that Janie has never backed away from any challenge. She took up golf at the comparatively late age of 13, and was further restricted in her development by the short playing season in her native New England. Once she felt the first tingle of excitement that tournament golf can offer, however, she set herself on a characteristically resolute course to become a great player.

I like the way Janie shares her tournament experiences with you in this book, in such a way that the amateur player can both relate and learn. Without the strong intention of producing instructional material, she offers some valid technical points. The putting chapter, in particular, can be enormously helpful to the average player.

The descriptions of life on tour and her analysis of rival players provide a penetrating view of the world of women's professional golf. I might add that the fact Janie competed as successfully as she did during the frustration of her problems with the LPGA is a testimonial in itself to her fighting instincts. The book's title, really, tells it all.

Janie will continue to grow as a tournament golfer. She has many great championships ahead of her. I think this was the ideal time in her career to write this book, and I know how eager she is to share her story with you.

As a friend I was gratified to see her triumph on the golf course. It was a vindication vital for Janie's personal career, and for all athletes who have been dealt with less than fairly under similar circumstances.

I commend her story to you. It offers a revealing insight into the life of a true golf champion, a professional athlete and a remarkable person. Share her story. Let it inspire your own endeavors.

—*Billie Jean King*

CONTENTS

Acknowledgements   5

Introduction by Billie Jean King   7

1. Go For It!   11

2. The Toski Touch   23

3. Life On The Tour   33

4. Sizing Up The Competition   49

5. On Trial   69

6. Fighting Back   93

7. Pressure Golf   103

8. On The Green: Women vs. Men   115

9. The Trouble With Women's Golf   123

10. New Competitive Challenges   133

11. The Future of Women's Sports   145

Career Record   157

1.

GO FOR IT!

I guess I've always been a fighter, going back to my early days in New Hampshire. I loved to compete. There was something about the challenge of competition that stimulated me, that forced me to play beyond my ability. I recognized it when I was playing on the boys' baseball team in grammar school. "Tomboy" Blalock, they called me, the kid who would grit her teeth and dig in when the going got tough.

After eight years on the women's professional golf tour, that competitive drive and urge to excel are still there. You cannot become a winner in any sport without them. And that's what this book is all about: *the guts to win*. The fire burns deeper in some of us. Sometimes it shows, sometimes it doesn't, but it's always there. I'll try to relate the problems I've faced on the golf course to yours, and I'll point out how you can overcome tension and fear with examples taken from my own experiences in professional golf.

Women have come a long way in sports during the last decade. Today, we female athletes have a new image and status that have enabled us to broaden the scope of our lives. I'm proud of the growth in women's professional golf and tennis, and of my involvement with women's professional softball. So I've tried to focus this book not only on my adventures in golf, but on the role that competition can play for all women athletes, professionals and amateurs.

People have told me I need a crisis to face before playing my best, and perhaps at one time that was true. Heaven knows, I've had my share of crises. It seems I've had to prove something for as long as I can remember. Adversity has been the story of my life.

There are times when I dread the pressure of tournament play, but I love it, too. That's probably why I enjoy so much the weekly competition of the women's tour. It's one battle after another. Good breaks are part of the picture, too. I can think of no better example than the first tournament I won as a professional.

It was August 9, 1970. We were playing the third and final round of the Lady Carling Open at the Indian Hills Country Club in Atlanta. I had joined the tour in May of 1969, and the rest of the year I managed to scrape out $3,825, which didn't do much more than meet expenses. Going into the Lady Carling I had earned just over $7,000 in 1970, considerably less than I had anticipated. I had been playing so poorly that, following the pro-am in Atlanta, I asked my good friend Jan Ferraris to take a look at my swing.

Jan, who had been on the tour for four years, was as helpful as ever. She noticed that I was taking the club back too much to the inside. I was swinging with my hands instead of my arms. This restricted swing, which I see so often in amateur golfers, was guaranteed to produce a hook under pressure. Jan got me to swing the club back on a straighter path, with full arm movement.

I started to hit the ball with more authority, but after two rounds of the tournament I had shot 74–77 and was five strokes behind the leader, Pam Barnett. I kept waiting for something to happen on the final round—one shot, one lucky break—that would put me in contention. I got two lucky breaks—on the sixth and seventh holes.

The sixth hole at Indian Hills is one of the toughest on the women's tour. It is a 390-yard par-4 with a sharp dogleg left. At the turn is a long fairway bunker on the left, as well as a creek which runs the entire length of the hole. The creek crosses to the right, in front of the elevated green which slopes left to right, perfect for plopping into the water. And, three bunkers surround the green.

I hit a good drive, and my 4-wood second shot wound up on the side of a mound. It was about 10 yards to the left of the green, not far from the water. I played an 8-iron chip shot that rolled into the cup for a birdie. That was the lift I needed. If you've competed in tournament golf, you know what something like that can do for your mental outlook. It gets the juices flowing. You can hardly wait to play the next hole.

The seventh hole at Indian Hills is a 180-yard par-3, the No. 1 handicap hole on the course. Both the tee and the green sit up on plateaus, separated by a shallow ravine. The two-tiered green is guarded on the front left and right by three traps. We were hitting into the wind. The girls had been averaging nearly four strokes on this hole during the tournament, so I figured a par would pick up a stroke on the field. What I had to do, then, was hit the green from the tee.

At that stage of my career I had trouble getting the ball into the air. I had to hit a high shot here, and I knew I couldn't do that with a quick, restricted swing. As I stood over the ball with a 4-wood, I concentrated on a slower, more complete backswing with a full shoulder turn. I was trying to make good, solid contact.

The shot covered the pin all the way. The gallery started to applaud when it landed, and then exploded into shouts and cheering. I had hit the ball into the cup! It was my first hole-in-one on the tour. I was in the fight now. I didn't know what the other girls were doing ahead of me or behind me, but I knew I had a chance to win the tournament.

I took over the lead on the ninth hole. Pam Barnett, playing behind me, had triple-bogeyed the sixth when she hit into a creek. The tournament was mine to win, if I could keep from blowing it down the stretch.

Under pressure, it's a constant struggle to maintain a full swing. The tendency is to restrict the backswing, to strike quickly at the ball. On the 17th, a straightaway par-4 of 380 yards, I succumbed to the pressure. I failed to complete my backswing, and swung with a hurried, jerky motion. What happened was inevitable—I hooked the ball into the woods.

Now was the time to see if I could fight back. I hit a wedge shot onto the fairway and was faced with a full 7-iron to the green. "People are expecting me to choke," I said to myself. "I'll show 'em." Taking a nice, full swing, I hit a 7-iron that landed three feet short of the hole and then rolled 20 feet past. I had a downhill putt, slippery and treacherous. The thing I most wanted to avoid was three-putting, so I stood over the ball until I had the distance clearly focused in my mind, and carefully stroked the ball. It fell into the cup on the last turn.

With that crisis behind me, there was no problem on the 18th. I hit a 3-wood off the tee and an 8-iron about 12 feet from the flag. I was nervous, of course, but I kept a good tempo on the putt. Although it lipped the cup and stayed out, I had a 70 for a score of 221. Now all I had to do was wait out all the others and see if my score would hold up.

Finally, it came down to whether Betsy Rawls could make a birdie putt of 30 feet on the 18th hole. She needed that to force us into a sudden-death playoff. One of the first things I learned in golf was that you don't ever root *against* anyone. Golf's not that kind of game. But in this case, I sure wasn't pulling for Betsy to make that putt. In the pictures taken there near the 18th green, I am leaning on Betty Burfeindt and Jan Ferraris with my head buried as Betsy lined up the putt. I couldn't bear to look.

Fortunately for me, Betsy's putt stopped eight inches short of the hole, and I had won my first LPGA tournament. What a feeling! Especially to win it the way I did—coming from five strokes back on the final round. The hole-in-one was a lucky shot, sure, but I had played some good, solid golf under pressure. I must have still been in a daze the next week at Cincinnati because I tied for last money and got a big fat check for $25.

I think the most important attribute in tournament golf is to recognize when you have the opportunity to win and then execute the shots required to do it. You aren't in contention every week, and when you are, you have to play that much harder. That applies to whether you're playing in a club event or on the professional tour.

Everybody gets excited in tournament golf. I've seen club golfers so tense they can hardly bring the club back. I try to overcome tension by taking some deep breaths, or by flopping my hands to keep the circulation flowing. There are times to play safe and times to gamble. You have to know what your own game can handle. Personally, I won't take a risk shot unless I have at least a 50–50 chance of pulling it off.

And here's another thing to consider. While the crunch is on, it is essential to maintain the same tempo you played with earlier in the round. The temptation, once your collar starts to tighten, is to play more conservatively and try to save what you have. It can't be done. I'm not talking here about taking stupid chances, like hitting a shot you really have no chance of pulling off. But if you're in contention late in the tournament, you must have done something right to get there. Maybe you gambled on reaching a par-5 hole in two by hitting a wood over water.

The agony of suspense. I can't bear to look as Betsy Rawls strokes her putt on the last hole of the 1970 Lady Carling Open

Now you have a chance to win, and the adrenalin is flowing. This is no time to lose your courage. I have a favorite saying: "Go for it." I'll give you a few examples of how that attitude really paid off for me.

The 1971 George Washington Classic was held at Horsham, Pa., a suburb of Philadelphia. I remember it well, because we played in brutally hot weather. It was like spending four hours in a blast furnace each day. It was so bad we had to use our umbrellas to block out the sun. During the second round, I suffered a heat stroke. I was seeing spots, and the ground seemed to be moving under me. Still, going into the final round, I was only two strokes behind the leader, Kathy Whitworth. Here was another chance to win.

On the first three holes of the final round I made birdie putts, really a good start. I had the bit in my teeth now, along with the lead. But on

in Atlanta. Betty Burfeindt and Jan Ferraris watch for me . . . and when Betsy misses, I win my first LPGA tournament!

the 16th, a par-5, I hit my drive up against a staked tree. I was nervous and excited, but was thinking clearly. Since the tree was staked, I was entitled to a free lift. It was a good omen. The ball could have landed up against any tree. Even though I had to drop the ball into the rough, I had a reasonably good lie. Good enough to go for it.

It had rained the night before, so I knew the traps were wet. The 16th green was guarded in the front by one of those wet traps. I was confident I could roll the ball through it. Making sure I stayed down through the shot, I dug the ball out of the rough with a 4-wood and rolled it right through the trap onto the green. Two putts later I had a very useful birdie.

The 17th was a par-3 hole with water on the left of the green. There are two ways to play that shot. You can go for the fat of the green or you can play for the pin, which on this day was tucked left. No question in my mind: I had to go for it. I hit a 4-iron shot that finished five feet away. I missed the putt, but I knew I was in good shape. On the final hole, with the pin in the upper right corner, I hit another 4-iron at the flag. Two putts later I had a 68 and the win.

I knew that I was not a good long-iron player. I couldn't get the ball high enough in the air with my tight, compact swing. I overcame that fault with lots of practice, working on a full, extended arm swing that produced a higher ball trajectory. It took several years before I had enough confidence in that shot to execute it under pressure.

Another situation where a gamble paid off occurred on the 72nd hole of the 1976 Carlton tournament at the Calabasas Country Club near Los Angeles. The purse of $205,000 was the biggest in LPGA history. Donna Young was running away with the tournament, on her home course, but second place was worth $22,000. That was $13,000 more than I received for winning by nine strokes at Dallas two weeks earlier. As we went into the last nine holes I looked at my caddie, Paul English, and said, "Now!" He knew what I meant. Blalock was going for it.

I birdied the 12th and got a key birdie on the 14th, a long par-3, by hitting a 3-iron two feet from the flag on a hole I had bogeyed three straight times. I saved par on 16 with a critical putt of five feet. I made a determined effort on that putt to keep my hands "quiet," my head still and just stroke it with my arms.

Going into the final hole, a par-5, Pat Bradley and I were one stroke behind Judy Rankin in the battle for second. It was a cold and windy day, the wind blowing left to right. I tried to get some extra distance off the tee and made the mistake of swinging too hard. I hit a drive that finished 15 yards short of my normal tee shot on that hole which meant 190 yards left to the front of the long, narrow green. With water hazards on the front right and along the left side, the green slopes left to right. I had a terrible lie, downhill and sidehill. Circumstances dictated a lay-up shot, playing for par, but I had been attacking the course throughout the back nine that day. I figured I could handle the situation. I went for it.

Aiming over the water to the left of the green, I took a slow backswing with the 3-wood and caught it flush, with just a slight fade. It carried to the green and finished on the right fringe. Judy also hit the green with her second. Pat, whose drive carried 20 yards past mine, laid up, as she frequently does in a tight situation. Judy three-putted for a par and Pat pitched on for her par. I got down in two putts for a birdie. That gave me a 69 and a total of 287 for a share of second place with Judy. Pat finished one stroke back.

That night I calculated that my 3-wood shot had been worth $10,000. It broke me out of the pack, and my check for $19,300 brought my total money winnings for the year to more than $90,000.

I certainly don't want to give the impression that I can pull those clutch shots out of my bag every time, like a magician. Lord knows, I've missed enough of them over the past eight years. And there have been times when I have chosen to play the conservative shot, as you should do when the situation dictates. But the only real way to win an LPGA tournament is to attack. The competition is so close and so intense that in the crucible of a close finish, you simply must put your cards on the table with an attacking shot.

Many times I have seen Sandra Haynie, who has as much guts as any player I know, hit a brassie from a tight lie in a crucial spot without a moment's hesitation or a flicker of fear. Sandra has enough faith in her ability to hit the shot that she will go for it and hang the consequences. That's the thin line that separates the winners from the losers on the professional tour.

You can see how important the right attitude is for any golfer. You've got to have a positive approach. Go with your best gun. For me it might mean leaning on a 3-wood in a tight lie, while for you it might mean hitting a 7-iron and then hitting a wedge. If your club has a water hazard in front of a tee that requires a carry of 130 yards, and the driver has you psyched, use the 4-iron off the tee. Whatever it takes to get the job done.

I suppose it's easy enough for me to say, but I do think you should remember that on an amateur level, golf is really just a game. The results of the match in a club tournament won't affect your bank account or precipitate a divorce, so go out and enjoy the competition. I guarantee you it's a lot more fun than what we go through during the last round of a tournament.

On the tour, there's no tomorrow after Sunday. Every shot magnifies in importance. You have to be mentally tough. That's when the fighting instinct comes out—when you must play every shot as though it means the tournament. I get good vibes on those Sunday rounds. It must be part of my makeup. There are times when I almost feel like an animal waiting to be turned loose from its cage.

My friend Joan Joyce, the great softball pitcher, summed it up rather well. I was playing in a tournament somewhere, I forget where, and I asked Joan, who was with me at the time, if she was going out to watch the first round. "No," she said. "It's boring to watch you on Friday and Saturday. I'll catch you Sunday, when the sparks fly."

One tournament I played with a Sunday attitude throughout was the 1971 Lady Pepsi at Indian Hills in Atlanta. The year before when I won, it had been called the Lady Carling. The name change didn't make any difference—it was still being played at Indian Hills, a course I regard with great fondness. I was leading the tournament late in the second round when a storm struck, and we sat in a shed just off the 16th fairway for two hours. I was hoping we'd get the round in, naturally, and finally we did. I took a two-shot lead into the last round.

The moment of truth for me that day came on the 14th hole, a par-5, reachable in two. The fairway cuts through the woods like a narrow ribbon. I hit a good drive, which put me into position to go for it. The problem was that slender fairway. You could go for a bundle of strokes in those trees. There was no point in dwelling on that, so I set up over the shot, glanced just once down the fairway, then hit. I reached the green and got the birdie. It was a big one, because coming into the last hole I was barely hanging on to a one-stroke lead.

The 18th green at Indian Hills is double-tiered and treacherous. I reached it with a drive and a 7-iron, but I had to run my first putt up that slope from 20 feet. It ghosted three feet past the cup. I set up firmly over the putt, took a short backswing and stroked it gently into the hole. I'd won another tournament by gambling when the situation arose. The attacking shot had once again paid off for me.

Later that evening, after a few beers in the clubhouse, a bunch of us went to the 18th green to see if I could make that last putt again. It was pitch dark, about midnight. We turned on the headlights of a car and began a little putting match. It was all pretty juvenile, I suppose. Anyway, we heard a gunshot and out of the woods swarmed a whole gang of security people armed to the teeth. They didn't know who we were, so they held us at gunpoint until someone from the club came out to identify us. Apparently, the club had been vandalized earlier in the year and they weren't taking any chances.

For all the importance of the weekly tour events, I don't suppose anything comes close to matching the significance of the Colgate-Dinah Shore Winners Circle. It's played each spring at the Mission Hills Country Club in Palm Springs, Calif., and for us gals it's the most important week of the year. The Colgate was the first women's tournament to offer a $100,000 purse. That was in 1972, when the men had been playing for that kind of money for years. It was a major breakthrough, thanks largely to the interest in the women's tour expressed by David Foster, chairman of the Colgate-Palmolive Company, which sponsors the event. I began thinking about that tournament the moment I holed my last putt of 1971.

In preparation for the Colgate, I worked with Tom Nieporte all during the winter of 1971–1972. Nieporte, a former touring pro, was teaching golf at the Royal Palm Course in Boca Raton, Fla. The practice range there is a quiet place away from all the traffic and hubbub of the club. We spent a lot of time playing shots in the wind, because Mission Hills is a windy course.

There are little tricks to playing on a breezy day and Tom knew them all. Normally, on a quiet day, I would hit a 7-iron on a 130-yard shot. Nieporte showed me how to get the same results from punching a 4- or 5-iron, while keeping the weight forward. You concentrate more on leading the club through the ball with the left hand, keeping it firm and hitting it with a crisper, more abbreviated technique. This results in a lower trajectory, which is exactly what you want on a course like Mission Hills when the wind starts whipping up.

I think that's a very good point for golfers of all levels to keep in mind. Controlling the shot is what you're after, and control can be ac-

My happy victory at the 1972 Dinah Shore: David Foster, chairman of the Colgate-Palmolive Company; Dinah, myself, Carol Mann and a disappointed Judy Rankin.

complished more easily by taking more club than the yardage dictates and swinging just a little easier. It's a point I often suggest to my partners in a pro-am.

To help strengthen my legs and build up my stamina, I took to running in the sand on the oceanfront just off the back door of my home in Highland Beach, Fla. That constant pounding up and down the beach aggravated a back problem I never realized I had, an inverted vertebra. It flared up whenever I tried to hit a golf shot. A doctor recommended laying off golf indefinitely, but the Colgate was coming up and I wanted desperately to play in it.

I arrived at Mission Hills on the Monday preceding the tournament, which that year was a 54-hole event. I hit an 8-iron shot off the practice tee that sent pain searing through my back. That night I had X-rays taken, and they showed a slight bone deformity in my back. I was immediately advised by the doctor to quit the tour for several weeks. He also told me that I might always have problems with my back.

"This is the biggest women's golf tournament in history," I told the doctor. "I've got to play. Can't you give me something that will allow me to swing for just this week? After that, I don't care what happens."

He gave me a cortisone shot, which requires 48 hours for maximum effectiveness. He also fitted me with a special back brace, a corset, really. Fortunately, the LPGA pairings committee gave me a late starting time on Wednesday for the first round of the two-day pro-am. This gave the cortisone enough time to take effect. Somehow I muddled through the 36 holes of the pro-am, but I still had 54 holes of competition ahead of me on a long and difficult course.

For the next three days I took two pain-killing pills each day and washed them down with a glass of milk. For me it was a new crisis, another chance to prove something.

On the final round, I was paired with Mickey Wright and Carol Mann. I had the feeling all week that most of the other women pros wanted the first Colgate to be won by a veteran player, someone who had helped build the LPGA through all the lean years. Carol was in position to win that last day. So was Judy Rankin. With two holes to go, I had a two-stroke lead.

The 17th at Mission Hills is a 180-yard par-3. The green is nearly 100 yards long, with a hump running vertically from front to back that makes it a terror to putt. The pin was placed in the upper right corner. With Mickey and Carol watching closely, I set up carefully over my 5-wood tee shot, took the club back slowly and hit the greatest clutch shot of my career up to that point. It finished eight feet from the pin. As we walked up to the green, Mickey told me that the shot actually gave her goose bumps. "I never knew," she said, "that you could produce such a fine shot under this kind of pressure."

I made the birdie putt and had a three-stroke lead going into the last hole, the first time I had ever enjoyed that luxury on the tour. The 18th is a par-5 that doglegs sharply left and plays to an island green surrounded by water. I hit my third shot, a 7-iron, onto the green. As I went past the huge gallery acknowledging the applause, and walked across the little bridge leading to the green, I felt warm waves of elation. I won the tournament by three shots, and the check of $20,000 was the largest a professional woman athlete had ever received in one event. I slept with that check under my pillow for a week.

A month later we were playing in the Suzuki Internationale, a $42,000 tournament at the Brookside course in Pasadena, right next to the Rose Bowl. What happened during that week proved to be the first indication of my future troubles with the LPGA—the first hint that 1972 would turn out to be my year of nightmare.

I got off to a good start with an opening round of 68. That put me one stroke behind Gloria Ehret, who was attempting to win her first tournament in six years. The next day I was paired with Ehret and

Joyce Kazmierski, who were then both slow players. I've always been a fast player, but the pace of your threesome is always dictated by the slowest one. We fell two holes behind the group ahead before we ever got to the turn. On the ninth tee we were informed by Gene McCauliff, the LPGA tournament director, that we each had been assessed a two-stroke penalty for not keeping up.

That really burned me up. There were, in fact, some valid reasons for our slow play. Joyce had hit a ball into the water on one hole, which meant she had to take off her shoes to play the shot, then dry her feet. Later on, Gloria knocked a shot up against a boundary fence, which ate up more time. I was smoldering over the penalty throughout the last 10 holes. I managed to shoot a 70, but without that two-stroke bump, I'd have been in the lead.

As I say, I've always been a fighter, and sometimes you have to do your fighting off the course. Right after the round, I protested that penalty. I pointed out the situations that created our delays and reminded McCauliff that he wasn't even out on the course to see what was going on. The penalty was rescinded. That night I heard some grousing from a few of the players who felt the penalty should have stuck. I should have realized right then that I was not the most popular woman on tour. Maybe I had been a little too successful that year.

Anyway, I went out the last day and played good, steady golf. Kathy Whitworth, who was paired a few groups ahead of me, shot a 67. That gave her a final score of 209, seven strokes under par. Standing on the 17th tee, I was also seven under.

The 17th at Brookside is a par-3 of about 150 yards. I hit a 5-iron off the tee that wound up 15 feet from the pin, then holed the putt for a birdie. All I had to do now was par the last hole to win.

After a fairly strong tee shot, I hit a 6-iron approach that finished 30 feet past the pin. My first putt was 3½ feet long. The tendency in that situation is to hurry the next putt, to get it over with as quickly as possible. But I forced myself to slow down and look it over carefully. It was almost as if I were walking on molasses. Everything seemed to take place in slow motion. Standing over the putt, I remembered to accelerate my left hand through the ball. I rolled it in for my par.

I had won my second tournament of the young season and I was on top of the world. Little did I know that a few weeks later that elation would shatter around me, like glass.

2.

THE TOSKI TOUCH

The first turning point in my golf career occurred on an April day in 1968, when I picked up the telephone in Pompano Beach, Fla., and called Bob Toski at the Ocean Reef Club in Key Largo. I had been spending a few weeks in Florida at the home of a college friend, Robbie Loehr. I had no money to play golf, so I would sneak out on the Pompano Beach Club for a few holes in the early evening. My game needed some help and Toski, then working at Ocean Reef, was building his reputation as one of the country's best golf teachers. I asked him if he would take a look at my swing.

Although he was polite, Toski had obviously never heard of me. Why should he? State and regional champions are seldom known beyond their home areas. I had failed to qualify for the only national event I had entered, the 1967 U.S. Women's Amateur. As Toski asked me some questions about my background, I became very nervous.

Finally he said, "Okay, come on over. Let's see what you can do."

Driving down to Key Largo, I was as jittery as a bride on her wedding day. I was about to take a lesson from Bob Toski—the guru of the golf swing, the Tommy Armour of his day.

Toski was smaller physically than I had expected, slender and wiry. As I hit a few shots, he stood there quietly. He prescribed a few things, and suggested I see him again the next day. He mentioned something about a total reconstruction of my swing.

Aware of his prestige as a teacher and having some idea about the kind of money he was getting from his pupils, I mumbled something about doubting whether I could afford his fee. "Don't worry about that," he said. "We'll talk about money later."

I did see him the following day, and for the next week I spent five hours daily commuting from Pompano Beach to Key Largo to work with him. Bob and I got along well. He wasn't kidding about a major overhaul of my swing. He said I was too mechanical, that I set up to hit the ball too far right of the target, that I had no arm motion and that I couldn't get the ball into the air. (Whenever I get together with Bob these days, he sends me into hysterics by imitating my early swing. It was the worst thing I've ever seen.)

My commute from Pompano Beach became too strenuous and eventually I rented a small kitchenette room in the Terrangi Motel in Key Largo. My room there cost $12 a week. Each night I would jam a chair up against the door because I didn't trust the lock. I ate my meals in the room. While I was cooking dinner one night, the stove blew up and I suffered some nasty burns on my hand and arm.

The Blalock family, golfers all. Brothers Jim (left) and Jack with Mom, Dad and myself spruced up for an evening out.

After about a week I was able to resume practice, and occasionally Toski and I would play a few holes together. "You've got a long way to go," he told me. "But you're a very determined girl. And you do have a remarkable ability to get the ball into the hole."

Toski changed just about every aspect of my game. He corrected my alignment, slowed my tempo and got me to swing the club back with more arm motion. He improved my putting stroke by making me accelerate the back of the left hand through the ball, and taught me to chip better by using the short takeaway with a firm-wristed stroke.

I learned how to practice with a purpose by working on certain things, such as tempo, rather than just standing out there beating balls. Toski showed me the importance of managing a round, of saving strokes by hitting away from trouble spots. If there was a big bunker guarding the front right corner of the green, he advised approaching to the left side. Things like that.

Toski never did charge me for that month of lessons, but he suggested I come back in the fall and work at the club while I continued my instruction. I got a room in the employees' quarters on the property, and did all sorts of odd jobs. I worked as a starter on the first tee, as a ranger to speed up play and I drove a tractor to pick up balls on the driving range. Sometimes at night the two pros, Mahrty Lehr and Melvin Deitch, and I would go out for a few "shooters" (cocktails) and have dinner at one of the great seafood restaurants in the Keys.

While I continued to work with Toski, I often acted as observer during his lessons with other pupils. That in itself was a great education. I was being exposed to golf on a daily basis, and I soaked it all in.

In January of 1969 I took a few days off to enter the Burdine's Invitational, a tour event, at Miami. I was still an amateur. My goal at that time was to play big-time amateur golf and make the U.S. team for the Curtis Cup. Imagine my astonishment when I finished fifth in the Burdine's! That really opened my eyes. The tournament was won by another amateur, JoAnne Carner, who turned pro the next year.

These were exciting times for a girl from New Hampshire who grew up idolizing athletes and who never picked up a golf club until she was 13. I did, however, have the advantage of growing up in a closely knit family atmosphere where sports were considered a natural outlet for a competitive child.

My dad, Richard Blalock, was the editor of the Portsmouth Herald until he retired a few years ago. He had played a little golf during his boyhood in St. Petersburg, Fla., but after moving to New Hampshire he was more interested in following the pro sports teams in Boston—the Red Sox, Bruins and Celtics.

Mom was a pretty good athlete, too. Her basketball coach at Penacook (N.H.) High School had been Red Rolfe, who was then playing third base for the New York Yankees during the baseball season. He spent his winters in Penacook and later coached at Dartmouth. Red taught me how to pitch, and I was good enough to play for the boys' team in grammar school.

I became a competitor early in life. Mom tells the story of the time, when I was about five, I started out the door wheeling a doll carriage. Instead of a doll, though, I had a large rock swathed in blankets. She asked me what I had in there.

"That's my in-casin' rock," I said.

"What's that?"

"That's in-casin' that mean boy up the street tries to bother me."

One Christmas my dad bought me a football helmet and shoulder pads, and my grandmother bought me a doll. The doll stayed in the closet.

When I was in junior high, a team of women basketball players of college age and older asked me to join them at the Portsmouth Com-

Tiger Blalock, front and center, with the Haven PTA grammar school baseball team in Portsmouth.

munity Center in a game against another town. There was a good-sized crowd on hand. With six seconds left and our team behind by one point, we called time. We set up a play that called for me to take the final shot. I put a jump shot through the basket and we won by a point.

I won the Portsmouth city candlepin bowling championship the same year, and that spring in a Junior Olympics field day I brought home all the blue ribbons. I felt a tremendous exhilaration in competing, and even then the will to win inside me was strong.

In art class one day the teacher asked us to draw a picture of the person who best typified the attitude we most admired. I drew my version of Jim Loscutoff, that demon competitor with the Boston Celtics. Loscutoff was a one-man demolition derby on the basketball floor. He'd take your head off to score a basket or grab a rebound. My picture was printed in the Celtics program.

In short, I was a rough, tough tomboy, and sports was my world. I used to dream about growing up to become a ballplayer.

Golf was another matter. Nobody paid much attention to golf in Portsmouth back then. The Portsmouth Country Club had been taken over by the Air Force during World War II, and it wasn't until many years later that the members built a new course. My parents took out a social membership.

When Mom was asked to enter a mother-daughter tournament, she borrowed an old set of clubs from a neighbor, Stan Maskwa, and bought me a new set. We hacked around in the event, and that night she announced her plans to take out a regular golf membership. "You can watch over your younger brothers when I play," she told me. "I've got a built-in baby sitter."

I began fooling around with my new clubs, hitting a few shots here and there. Stan Maskwa took me out for a round. I remember his first words. "In this game, Janie," he told me, "you've got to grind away. When the going gets tough, keep grinding." That night I told Mom to look for another baby sitter. I had discovered a new sport.

That summer, when I was 13, I entered my first tournament. It was a nine-hole event for junior girls at the Beaver Meadow Country Club in Concord. On the way to the course my mom, knowing how I hated to lose in anything, tried to counsel me. "Don't be discouraged if you do badly," she said. "Golf is a difficult game."

There were 15 junior girls in the tournament. I shot 49 and brought home the first-place trophy. The game was seeping into my blood.

The women members of the New Hampshire Golf Association let me play with them in their Tuesday events. Two teachers at the University of New Hampshire, Joan Stone and Jackie Clifford, were 5-handicap players. Since the university was only 10 miles from Portsmouth, they came over to practice and play frequently at our club. I used to watch them, and occasionally they would invite me to play. I was nervous in that distinguished company, but I always learned something about golf.

By the time I was 17, I had won two State Junior Girls championships and was shooting consistently in the mid-80s. I entered the Portsmouth Women's Club Championship, reaching the finals. I was five holes down with six to play, then I remembered Stan Maskwa's words about "grinding" and I carried the match to the 18th hole. My parents were so pleased they gave me a new golf bag.

Branching out, I won the New England Junior in 1963 when I was 18. One of the players I beat was Suzy Chaffee, the skier from Rutland, Vt. I lost in the final of the New Hampshire Women's Amateur that year to Joan Stone, but I came back to win it four straight times.

I learned a few things about match play golf in those tournaments—things that could be useful to golfers at all levels. For example, there's a tendency in a match to tighten up whenever you lose a hole early in the competition. Anxiety leads to tension, and tension eats away at your game.

In an 18-hole match, you have a lot of time to win. Falling behind early only means that you have a little ground to make up. It often means also that you have a few good breaks coming your way. Be pa-

tient. Wait for them, and when they occur, make your move. I've been in more than one match where I lost four of the first five holes and still won. I'm never afraid now when I fall behind early in a tournament, in match play or stroke play. Breaks even out.

Another discovery I made early in my golf career was that so many of my opponents always seemed to play their best against me. I can only take that as a compliment. When Bobby Jones was playing in a match tournament, he never wanted to hear how badly his next opponent had played the day before. All he wanted to know was what score his opponent was capable of shooting on his best day. Jones always figured that best day might come in the match against him.

Although I still think stroke play is by far the better test of golf, match play is a great format for the competitive player. You often can size up your opponent just by looking him or her in the eye on the first tee. I learned to survive in match play not long after I took up the game, by playing my dad for a dime a hole. Dad has been a 15-handicapper for a long time. He hits the ball a mile, but never knows where it's going. I earned my allowance as a youngster by taking him for 40 or 50 cents after school in the afternoon.

My family still likes to play golf together, although Mom always claims she's out of practice. Both of my brothers are excellent golfers, shooting in the 70s. Jack, 25, runs our family restaurant, the Olde Ferry Landing, in Portsmouth. We opened it in the summer of 1975 and I still like to put on my apron and wait on tables. The seafood is outstanding. My younger brother Jim, 23, is now a graduate student at Rollins College.

I went to Rollins, too, because I wanted to get away from those harsh New England winters. Located in Winter Park, Fla., a suburb of Orlando, Rollins has a beautiful campus that captivated me on my first visit. I had earlier considered Duke or Wake Forest.

When I enrolled at Rollins, the school didn't have a women's golf team. We created our own. I didn't have a scholarship, either. I did meet some of the greatest girls anywhere. Wendy Overton, now a professional tennis player, was my roommate. Debbie Austin, a current regular on the tour, was probably the best female golfer in school at that time, although Wendy wasn't bad. As for me, my Toski days were ahead of me, so I couldn't really consider myself a player. Not yet.

Golf wasn't my only competitive outlet. I played on my Kappa Kappa Gamma sorority teams and we never lost a game in four years in basketball, volleyball and softball. I was the sorority's all-time scoring champion in basketball. After I graduated, Kappa Kappa Gamma took the tennis shoes I had worn for four years and had them bronzed. They are still there, in the sorority's trophy case.

I majored in history and got my degree in 1967. That fall, with nothing better to do, I lived at home in Portsmouth and substituted as a high school history teacher. Mostly I skied—and thought about golf.

In the spring of 1968 my mother could take it no longer. "You're

My first golf trophy at age 13, the result of a sparkling 49 in a nine-hole junior tournament at Beaver Meadow C.C.

restless, Janie," she remarked. "And you're bored. It's obvious you don't want to teach school for a living. You love golf, but you've never really given it a chance. Why don't you go back to Florida so you can play golf every day?"

I made arrangements to stay with Robbie Loehr's parents in Pompano Beach, my folks loaned me some money and within a few days I was on my way. That's when Bob Toski came into my life.

Fortified with my first wave of Toski teachings, I returned home in the summer of 1968 to play tournament golf. The Eastern Women's Amateur was held that year at the Rhode Island Country Club. The winner was JoAnne Carner. I finished second.

I also had my first exposure to the U.S. Women's Open that year, and what an unpleasant memory that was. It was played at the Moselem Springs Country Club, near Reading, Pa. I drove to the tournament in my convertible and stayed in a private home. After shooting 80 in the first round, I was driving back to the house when I passed a girl who was cutting her lawn with a rotary mower. A rock got caught in the blades, flew up and struck me in the face. It was a freak accident, but I was lucky not to lose an eye.

My hosts took me to a doctor who sewed me up, without benefit of an anesthetic. With severe facial lacerations and a triple fracture of the cheekbone, I was through with tournament golf for the summer. I returned home looking like a mummy.

When I finished fifth in the Burdine's tournament in January 1969, I got to thinking seriously about a career in professional golf. Jan Ferraris, who joined the tour in 1966, said I had the game to win some prize money right away. "But I don't think you'll turn pro," she told me. "You're not ready yet to make that decision."

Well, there was another challenge. What did she mean, I wasn't ready to make that decision? Was she really saying I didn't have the guts to make it? It was like taunting a bull with a red flag. So long, Curtis Cup dreams.

I kept my amateur status for the next few months. In the spring I entered the Women's North and South, a big match play tournament at Pinehurst. The night before I played Barb McIntire in the final, I wrote the U.S. Golf Association declaring my intentions to turn pro. But it was such a big step I couldn't mail the letter myself. Jan Ferraris mailed it for me on the morning of the final, which I lost to Barb. That was my last competition as an amateur.

My life seems full of ironies. I broke in on the pro tour with a 13th-place finish and won a check of $240. Guess where? In the Bluegrass Invitational at Louisville, the same place where I would be called before a group of my fellow players one horrible night three years later, accused of cheating.

That's me at 15, on the day I upset the defending champion, Pat McGahey, in the New Hampshire State Women's Amateur.

3.

LIFE ON THE TOUR

The next time you're browsing through the Monday morning sports section of your newspaper, check the summaries of the weekend's LPGA tournament with an eye toward a sudden change in scores. If a player shot something like 71-70-80, it doesn't necessarily mean that she wilted under the pressure of the final round. More than likely it means that Sunday was the first day of her monthly menstrual cycle.

I've never seen this subject brought up in a golf book, but it's definitely a factor in our life on the tour. We all live with it, and we discuss it freely among ourselves. The first time I heard it mentioned was during my early days on tour. Donna Caponi, after leading through 36 holes, shot a high round on Sunday. I kiddingly asked her if she had choked. "Nope," Donna replied. "I got my period."

It's no laughing matter for the women who make their living on the golf course. On those days it can be torture to play. Not only can the cramps be extremely uncomfortable, the additional fluid in your system takes away all sense of feeling in your hands. The putting stroke becomes jerky, and the finely grooved timing in your shotmaking goes out of whack. This is a problem that has affected all women on the course at one time or another. Is there any solution?

I've never been one to take a lot of corrective medication, but some women pros have found relief in water pills. Others use aspirin. I just mostly suffer. One thing I do try is to keep my timing as slow and methodical as possible. I take the club back with a slower tempo, and I try to minimize the inevitable quickness in my putting stroke.

At the beginning of each season, I look over the schedule and try to estimate when my monthly will fall. I avoid playing that week whenever possible, but I hate to pass up a big tournament. Last year it struck me on the first day of the Carlton, our biggest event of the season with a $205,000 purse. I scraped it around in 77 that day, struggling on every shot, but came back with good rounds after that to finish in a tie for second place and collect a check for $19,300.

Another female-type problem is encountered by those women players who are generously endowed. The golf swing was not constructed for the full-figured woman. Did you ever hear of Anita Ekberg playing golf?

In the instructional schools they teach the woman with an ample chest to bend more at the hips, clearing the way for the swing. I'd agree with that. Our most prominent example on tour is Penny Pulz, who came over from Australia. Penny holds her hands quite a bit higher on the setup, so her front won't interfere with the swing. Some of

Pro-am time in Montreal with my girlhood idol, the mustachioed and determined-looking Bobby Orr, then of the Boston Bruins.

the women I've seen in club events might consider doing the same thing.

As long as we're involved in these personal matters, I think it's time we discussed the subject of lesbianism on the women's tour. It's something we hear a lot about, mostly from ill-informed people who are eager to perpetuate an old myth. Years ago, the woman athlete was often stereotyped as a lesbian, whether it was true or not. She looked tougher and less feminine than most women, and, in fact, was probably stronger and better developed muscularly. Because of that it was assumed that she had masculine characteristics.

Thus, some of the women who played the tour in the early days were stuck with this image, and the public came to associate them with female homosexuals. We hear it today, even though the appearance of women golfers has changed. One reason why the charge of lesbianism is so often leveled at women on the pro tour is that we spend so much time together. We travel together, and many times we room together. This creates, in the minds of many people, an abnormal relationship. Well, life on the tour is abnormal to some extent. Our home is on the road. We have no real roots. The guys we meet are here one week, gone the next, so we turn to each other for companionship, for someone we can confide in.

People see this and they criticize us for it. But what about the men's tour? The men share expenses by traveling together and they share their loneliness by dining with other men. Why don't people accuse them of homosexuality?

While the public is slowly acknowledging the existence of the gay person, the time is not yet ripe for open acceptance of a gay relationship. This is particularly true in golf. Golf is an established sport, played largely by establishment people. They do not seem to understand that few people are truly happy, and that some must reach out for happiness in a way the average person does not comprehend.

The friendships on the women's tour arise out of loneliness and need. There are, after all, different types of love. It need not be sexual. I have a feeling of love for Jan Ferraris, and I love the girls on the softball team Billie Jean King and I started a few years ago. That doesn't mean I go to bed with them.

My own personal view is that I don't care what kind of a relationship the girls might have on the tour. Sexual preference really is a personal thing. It doesn't affect my feelings for anyone. I also believe the percentage of lesbianism on the tour is no greater than in any other group of 100 women traveling on the same circuit. We have it to some degree, but is it more than a traveling tennis troupe, a cast of ice skaters or a circus? I don't think so.

The truth is that women golfers are becoming more and more desirable as females. The phones are ringing off the hooks in our motels, and the callers are men. You ought to see some of the male groupies who follow us around week after week. They like to be around celebrities, and the girls playing the tour have become celebrities. We've had lively pro-am parties at many tournaments leading to an equal number of propositions and proposals. It happens all the time.

My interest in the opposite sex began many years ago. During my last two years in high school and my freshman year at Rollins, I dated a boy from my home area named Dick Lyczak. He went to college at Dartmouth. We talked about getting married some day, but I chose to give my golf career top priority. I remember telling him I'd quit golf when I won the New Hampshire State Women's Amateur. I hadn't seen Dick Lyczak in years, but I recently met him while playing in Hong Kong, where he is now teaching psychology.

In 1967, while competing in the Women's Trans-Mississippi amateur tournament at Rochester, Minn., I met another neat guy. His name was Dave Schraeder. He was an intern at the Mayo Clinic in Rochester. We had some great times together that week, and we corresponded for awhile. Then he stopped writing. I waited for the letter that never came. I've often wondered what happened to him.

A few years later, I began to see quite a bit of Clyde Genz, who lives in Boca Raton, not far from my home in Highland Beach. Clyde advised me on a number of financial matters, and we became good friends. One day I introduced Clyde to Sandra Palmer, and they quickly became good friends. I don't see much of him anymore.

For a brief time several years ago, I seemed to be on a hockey kick. Being a New Englander, I had always followed hockey, especially the Boston Bruins. My all-time favorite athlete is Bobby Orr, who was then a superstar with the Bruins (before being traded to the Chicago Black Hawks in 1976). We were playing a tournament in Montreal, and when my caddie picked me up at the airport he said, "I've got a surprise for you. You're playing with Bobby Orr in the pro-am." Well, I couldn't get over that. It was too much.

There was a message at my hotel that Bob Orr had called and left a number. I returned the call. We had a nice chat, although I was so excited I could hardly concentrate on what was being said. We had a super time on the course the next day. That night I joined Bobby and some other hockey players for drinks and then I had dinner with Bobby before he had to catch a late flight out.

Rick Martin of the Buffalo Sabres, who was also in town for the pro-am, also came into the picture. We became pretty good friends. When we were playing in a tournament at Buffalo later on, I saw quite a bit more of Rick.

I also became good friends with Dan Pastorini, quarterback of the Houston Oilers, during a pro-am in Houston, and did some socializing with Rod Gilbert, the New York Ranger hockey star, after a pro-am in Las Vegas.

Successful athletes seem to have a common bond. They're really very special people. They're not so caught up in their own world that they don't have time for other people.

Another interesting aspect of the tour is the male caddie. No description of tour life would be complete without mentioning him. The men have had more or less permanent caddies on their tour for a long time, but this is a fairly recent phenomenon among the women. We competed for years under the restriction that you couldn't use the same caddie for more than three weeks in a row. That's been changed and, as a result, there have been some real characters who have emerged as components of the tour.

Where they came from I really don't know. They just sort of appeared on the scene several years ago, when we were allowed permanent caddies. There are about 30 of them currently traveling our tour, most of them averaging about $200 a week, plus a share of the pot if you finish high in a tournament. They pay their own expenses, so they can't wind up with much at the end of the year; but they like the life and I think they add a lot to the flavor of the tour.

Another pro-am, another celebrity partner: Dan Pastorini, the handsome quarterback of the Houston Oilers. This is work?

Most of these caddies stay together, three or four in a room, usually at a different motel than the golfers. I've heard they get some lively poker games going at night, and they have some interesting bets going on each day's play. "I'll take my 'horse' for $25 this round against yours," that sort of thing. I don't know when my caddie places a bet on me and I don't want to know, but it's common knowledge that they do.

These fellows are usually known only by their first names or nicknames. Carol Mann has a caddie named Rat. Mary Bea Porter prefers one called Rabbit, but not the same Rabbit who caddies for Gary Player. Kathy McMullen often uses Richie, who sports an impressive mustache. Roscoe has done a good job for Jan Ferraris. Pepper, Runt and Mule have worked for several girls. Judy Rankin has worked recently with Red. Judy's former caddie was Billy Prentice, Jo Ann's nephew, but he was fired by Yippy, Judy's husband. And so it goes.

The best caddie I've had is Paul English, a young man from Rhode Island who has carried my bag for two years. I picked Paul up shortly after he was fired by Don Carner, JoAnne's husband. As you can see, husbands often get into the act. Their wives might not have any major gripes about their caddies, but if Yippy Rankin or Don Carner or Bill Cornelius takes a dislike to him, he's gone.

The caddies arrive at a tournament course a couple of days ahead of the golfers. Their basic duty during this time is to get the distances from prominent landmarks, such as a big tree or a water nozzle, to the front of the green. They call this "marking off the course." We use the front of the green as a guideline, because we get to know the characteristics of each green during the practice rounds. They also give us a chart before each tournament round showing the location of each pin placement. When the caddie tells you it's 140 yards to the front of the green, you consult the pin placement and determine the additional yardage. It's a good system.

On my final practice round, I like to run a little spot check on distances to see how mine coincide with my caddie's. I've found that a caddie such as Paul English is usually very accurate. If there's any slight discrepancy in yardage, I split the difference.

My demands of a tour caddie are pretty basic. I want him right there with the bag, so I don't have to wait. I don't want much conversation or any display of emotion. I get angry enough at myself without having the caddie grumbling over a bad break. I don't want him to touch the club, either. I make the selection, based on our yardage chart and the wind, and then I take the club out of the bag myself. Once I'm lining up the shot, I tell him not to say a word. There's nothing more distracting than standing over the ball while your caddie is carrying on a one-way conversation in the background.

I'll consult with the caddie on the greens over the break of the putt, but mostly I'll rely on my own judgment. That way, if I mis-read the green, I have nobody to blame but myself.

It seems to me that women playing in club events on their home course, or even at courses they are unfamiliar with, can use their caddies more extensively than we do on tour. Caddies who spend their summers working at one club are usually very knowledgeable about the course. They can be a great help, not only in determining distance but in reading the greens. There are caddies at my old home course in Portsmouth who literally know every blade of grass. One of them is

On the job with my favorite caddie, Paul English. Notice that I'm taking the club out of the bag myself. It's something I always do.

John O'Leary, called "Meatwagon" by all the Portsmouth members.

Our lifestyle on the tour varies in direct proportion to our money winnings. It also varies with the existence, or lack, of a sponsor. I never had one, but I can tell you something about what they do. Say that a young pro has earned her playing card at the LPGA Qualifying School, held just before the start of each season. A businessman from her home town, or a group of businessmen, back her for the first year of competition. The usual stake is $15,000, which covers the bulk of the rookie's expenses for the year. She repays the sponsor or sponsoring group through a contractual arrangement that generally calls for the golfer to keep 40 percent of her money winnings, if there are any.

Most of the young pros today have sponsors. I don't know how they could get along without one, considering the high cost of travel and the intense competition. I started out in 1969 with a bankroll of $1,000, a combination of my own meager savings and a loan from my parents. I made less than $4,000 that first year and came out about even.

My $1,000 stake had dwindled to almost nothing by the middle of that first year. Right after the Borden Classic in Columbus, before we left for the U.S. Women's Open in Pensacola, I had to borrow $500 from Jan Ferraris. I charged my plane ticket, without having enough money in the bank to cover it. Fortunately, I won some money at Pensacola, paid Jan back and have never had any serious money worries since.

When you're on the lower strata of the tour you can get by for about $150 a week. These days it costs me between $600 and $800 for an average week on the tour, and my caddie gets another 10 percent of my earnings.

Thinking back on that first year, it was fun but a hectic way to live. Jan Ferraris and I bought a new Ford and we put 30,000 miles on it in one year. We always packed on Saturday night so we could take off down the road as soon as we had both finished play on Sunday. We'd throw our clubs into the trunk and drive four or five hours, until we spotted a place both of us considered economical enough. We ate a lot of hamburgers and hot dogs.

Many of the girls still travel by car, but in 1971 I began to fly from city to city. I found it was a lot easier on the nerves. On the longer trips I like to fly first class. Flying in the front cabin is not only more comfortable, because it gives me a better chance to stretch my long legs, it also gives me a better feeling about myself. I perform better on the course. It's probably an ego thing, but I'll continue to do it as long as I can afford the cost. My air travel bill for the year is about $9,000, which doesn't include the foreign trips for which our transportation is paid by the sponsor.

Another luxury I grant myself now is rooming alone. I used to share a room with Jan Ferraris. Jan comes from a fine family. Her father, Richie Ferraris, leads the band that plays on the top floor of the Francis Drake Hotel in San Francisco. Jan was a good roommate, and I still

Early days on tour with Jan Ferraris and our Jaguar with the "Choke" license plate that got a laugh wherever we traveled.

stay in her townhouse in Palm Springs during the Dinah Shore tournament. But I have become an independent cuss and I enjoy the freedom of my own room on the regular tour stops.

Speaking of Richie Ferraris, he came out to watch Jan and me play in a California tournament during my rookie year. I guess he wasn't too impressed with me. "Do Janie a favor," he told Jan. "Tell her to get off the tour. Nobody who swings like Shirley Temple can make a living in this game."

For the next couple of years, he always jokingly called me "Shirley Temple." I'd laugh, and tell him to stick to leading a band.

After awhile the motel rooms and the restaurants look pretty much alike. The best commercial place we stay at is Nendell's Inn in Portland, Ore. It has a ski lodge atmosphere, but it's really a family spot and serves great seafood. The most enjoyable weeks are spent in private homes, with friends. Nick and Jane Agati, who live in Atlanta, offered their home during my rookie year on the tour to "any poor girl who can't afford a motel room." Actually, their home turned into a palace of champions in Atlanta. I won twice while I stayed there; and Jan Ferraris and Betty Burfeindt each won once. The Agatis serve the finest spaghetti to be found anywhere.

The Dinah Shore is our favorite tournament, not only because of the big purse and the fun atmosphere at Mission Hills, but because Palm Springs is home to so many of the touring pros. Sandra Palmer and I jointly own a home there, which she has sort of taken over. It's been a lucky place for us. I stayed there in 1972, the year I won, and again in 1974, when I lost in the playoff to Jo Ann Prentice. Sandra stayed there during the 1975 tournament that she won. Jan Stephenson, who also lives in Palm Springs, made a great showing in the 1976 Dinah Shore, getting more television footage than anyone.

My routine has changed a little in the last year or so. I like to get away from golf for a couple of days now, flying up to Connecticut on Mondays whenever possible to be with the softball team. If I do come into a tournament town on Tuesdays, I like to reserve that day for fun things like shopping and a nice long lunch. I usually don't get out to the course until Wednesday for the pro-am, when I check my yardages and get a general feel for the course. I'll play a practice round on Thursday and spend some extra time hitting balls. I want to be ready when the bell rings on Friday.

On tournament days the normal routine is to eat just two meals a day, one of them occasionally a leftover from the night before. When I'm teeing off between 10 a.m. and 1 p.m., as I generally do, I'll get up early and have as big a breakfast as possible. Ham, eggs, a steak I saved in a doggie bag from last night's dinner, toast and plenty of orange juice. I won't eat again until that evening, either a dinner with friends in a good restaurant or a meal in my room while watching television.

Most of the tournaments provide courtesy car service from the motel to the course. That's a nice gesture, but I prefer to rent a car. Instead of waiting around for the courtesy car to show up, I can leave whenever I want. Allowing for normal traffic, which in some places like Los Angeles requires plenty of leeway, I try to arrive at the course exactly one hour ahead of my starting time. I check for mail in the players' locker room, take a good workout on the practice tee and putt for about 15 minutes before showing up on the first tee.

Once the round is over, I do my best to leave it at the course. I like to unwind right away with a beer at the clubhouse. In my sophomore year at Rollins, I was elected into a group whose official designation was the "Honorary Society of Hell Raisers." Thinking back, I met all the requirements. I drank enough beer to last me a lifetime. I never quite got over the habit; I still like a cold one from time to time.

One thing I don't like to do is sit around and make small talk. That seems such a waste of time. I like serious discussions on politics, philosophy or social issues that confront the country. Anything that is guaranteed to get your mind off golf.

In the past few years I've done quite a bit of foreign travel, partially because of the Colgate tournaments that have taken us to Australia, the Philippines and Europe. In 1973 I was invited to participate in the World Ladies Golf Classic at the Yomiuri Golf Club in Tokyo.

As you may have heard, the Japanese are attracted to Americans with fair complexions. They are crazy about Jack Nicklaus, Johnny Miller and Laura Baugh. Laura is probably better known in Japan than she is in the United States. Anyway, the promoters over there wanted 10 American women pros for the 1973 tournament. They worked through an American agent, Ed Barner of Los Angeles, who contacted me. The financial arrangements, including expenses and appearance money, were good. Over and above the guarantee, you kept whatever you earned.

I didn't win that year, but in 1975 I did, after I almost had heart failure on the last hole. It's a long par-3, which I barely reached with a driver. I had a two-stroke lead at the time that looked like a lock, especially when Sayo Yamasaki, who was two strokes behind me, hit her tee shot into a trap 50 yards to the right of the green. She proceeded to hole the bunker shot for a deuce, and I had to get down in two putts from 50 feet to win. My second putt was an uphill four-footer. I said to myself, "Don't quit on the stroke. Get your hands through the ball." I stroked it firmly into the cup and became the champion of the 1975 World Ladies Golf Classic, which included a check for a lot of yen that translated into 7,000 American dollars. The flight home was most enjoyable.

Through trial and error I have learned how to pack for the tour. I travel much lighter now than I once did. Jeans have been partially responsible for that. I wear them almost everywhere off the course. I build my tournament outfits around sleeveless blouses, slacks and a collection of six sweaters that I can match up with anything. I like to wear short shorts — hot pants, if you will — preferably an Oleg Cassini line made by Munsingwear. They have become my trademark, along with the pigtails. You need some indentifiable stripes in this business. Why do you think Sam Snead has worn straw hats all these years?

At the start of each season I make certain to buy a new suitcase. It gives me a lift, something to signify a new year. I never wear the luggage out in one season, but whenever the tour gets underway each January in Florida, I simply must have that new suitcase.

From the day that I joined the tour in 1969, I kept hearing about how much extra money the better players could make off the course. Exhibitions, endorsements, club and resort affiliations — these were all supposed to be gold mines waiting for us to come along and tap them. The way to do that, of course, was through a business manager or agent. I was told that no successful woman pro should be without one.

Despite the fact that I was Rookie of the Year in 1969 and was named Most Improved Player in both 1970 and 1971, I didn't believe I was generating enough commercial business to afford the luxury of a manager. But one day in 1972 I was watching my old Rollins roommate, Wendy Overton, play tennis at the Boca Raton Hotel. Wendy introduced me to Billie Jean King, and the next day we played golf.

"You ought to get some kind of a deal where you would represent a golf resort on tour," Billie Jean told me. I replied that nobody seemed to be breaking down the doors. Billie Jean mentioned casually that her husband Larry frequently jogged with Dick Butera, president of the Hilton Head Co., which operated the big new resort hotel in South Carolina. I picked Billie Jean's brains throughout the round, trying to learn more about Hilton Head. She promised to talk to Larry, who got back to me a little later.

Larry did much of Billie Jean's promotional work. He was familiar with contracts and how they were set up, and the deal he made for me sounded very good. First, I was to help design a new course they were building at Hilton Head. I was also to represent Hilton Head on tour. My remuneration was going to be $10,000 a year and a condominium at the resort.

I made a couple of trips to Hilton Head, paying my own expenses, to meet with the people there. I also signed a contract, but learned later that the contract had never been signed by Hilton Head. I represented that club for a year on the tour. Ray Scott, who did the telecast at one of our tournaments, identified me as Hilton Head's playing pro, which was a tremendous plug for the resort.

It ended with a dull thump. Instead of the $10,000 yearly retainer, I received a $3,000 settlement from Hilton Head, and never did get my condominium. One of Larry King's agents took 20 percent of that $3,000. When Larry set up his own company called Future, Inc., a year later, he signed Sandra Palmer. It was the start of a painful series of misadventures and misunderstandings with agents.

I was really desperate. Other girls were making good money on their business deals and I was making nothing. The word got around that Laura Baugh was pulling in $300,000 a year from her affiliation with Mark McCormack, the Cleveland attorney who had become the No. 1 sports agent in the country. I thought that if he was that good for Laura he ought to have something for me, too, so I signed with Mark early in 1975. He was to get 25 percent of what he generated for me off the golf course, plus 10 percent of my money winnings on tour.

The deal didn't work out at all. McCormack reneged on some promises, I felt, and petty irritations kept cropping up. For example, I was charged 61 cents for a wire involving a deal on a watch. I also had to pay a penalty on my income tax because McCormack's people were late in filing for an extension.

Mark now claims that most women pros are difficult to work with,

Checking the yardage in Japan. My little caddie can't speak English, but she's obviously got something to say.

45

which I don't think is true. The fact is that within the last 18 months several of the better players who had been clients, including me, have left him.

Meanwhile, through my friendship with Wendy, I began working on a deal with The Swallows, a golf and tennis complex in Florida. The day after I won the Lady Errol near Orlando I met with the Swallows people. I haven't heard from them since.

That was really a blow, because I had turned down an opportunity to represent Bonaventure, a golf club just off Alligator Alley in Florida, to go with The Swallows. Jack Gaines, who also ran Inverrary Country Club in Florida, was heading up the Bonaventure operation. I know Jack, and should have signed with him. Isn't hindsight beautiful?

There's more. During the off-season I often play at The Hamlet of Delray Beach, located just a few miles from my home at Highland Beach. Laura Baugh was representing The Hamlet on tour, but she was also affiliated with Canyon Country Club in Palm Springs. Pete Kelly, who was heading up the financing for the purchase of The Hamlet, talked with me one day about an affiliation. I was all excited about the prospect. That was the last I ever heard about it.

I also had some conversations with Delta Airlines about representing that company on tour, which would have been a terrific deal for me. That cooled off and died around the time of my legal problems with the LPGA. I still fly Delta occasionally—but I pay my own way.

My association with Mark McCormack lasted one year. One of the deals he did arrange for me was to play in a series of three exhibitions with men and women pros at Geneva in the summer of 1975. Gary Player and Bobby Cole, both McCormack men, were involved. I had planned to fly over early and spend some time prior to the Geneva matches in London, watching Billie Jean King play at Wimbledon.

There was one complication. I had a release from the tour event in Wheeling, W. Va., which was scheduled the same week as the tennis at Wimbledon. But I learned that five other players would not be given their releases unless I participated in the pro-am. So I flew from Miami to Pittsburgh, rented a car and drove to Wheeling. I pulled up at the golf course just before my 8 a.m. starting time in the pro-am. Nobody even knew I was there, except my three playing partners.

As the day dragged on, I knew it would be impossible to complete the round, drive back to Pittsburgh and catch my night flight to London out of New York. After 16 holes I simply said, "Fellas, I've got to go." My partners were very nice about it. I roared out of town and caught my flight. I spent two days at Wimbledon, watching Billie Jean win the women's singles, then flew off to Geneva.

There was a happy sequel to the Wheeling incident. The next year I returned there and won the tournament in a sudden-death playoff with Pat Bradley.

Meanwhile, I finally found a good business manager, an attorney from Syracuse, N.Y., named Tony Rivizzigno. Things are working out well. Tony has lined up several exhibitions and signed me to some profitable endorsements. So hopefully all that travail will pay off yet. I have many years ahead of me on the tour, and there are sizable amounts of money to be made off the golf course.

In 1976, following my best season on the tour so far, I took some time off and enjoyed my first real vacation in years. I visited with my parents in New Hampshire, worked on this book and spent a few weeks tuning up on the practice tee for tournaments in the Philippines and Hong Kong.

It's really not a bad life.

4.

SIZING UP THE COMPETITION

I've always thought of the women's tour as sort of a microcosm of the world we live in. We have all types out here, believe me. We spend so much of our time together that we get to know each other rather well. Like anywhere else, the tour has good people and also the kind I prefer to avoid. I'd like to share my opinions of both kinds with you.

The finest woman golfer over the past decade, without any question, has been Kathy Whitworth. She has won over 75 tournaments and nine times in her career has been the leading money winner. Kathy has to rank with the greatest athletes of all time, male or female. Unfortunately, hardly anyone outside of golf knows who she is.

Kathy's problem is that she lacks what the American sporting public calls charisma. That's a difficult quality to define, except to say that some athletes, such as Arnold Palmer, have it. Others do not. I don't believe it is anything that can be acquired, like a suntan or bright teeth. You simply have it or you don't. Kathy, for all her great skill on the golf course, does not.

While this has penalized Kathy financially in terms of commercial appeal, the biggest victim has been the LPGA itself. For years the tour was crying out for a superstar with personality, someone who could win tournaments and sell women's golf at the same time. Like Babe Zaharias and Patty Berg of other eras. Players like that could have been a tremendous asset to the LPGA. Kathy wasn't the person.

It wasn't her fault, of course. She worked hard to promote the LPGA. She won all those tournaments and said all the right things at the presentation ceremonies and never caused anybody any problems. But think where women's golf would be today had a female Arnold Palmer come along 10 years ago, one who could win 75 tournaments and also make everyone aware that she was in town.

I enjoy being paired with Kathy, mostly for the opportunity it affords of observing her skill at close range. She is not an exciting player to watch or an exciting person to be around. She's quite negative about many things. She often puts herself down, and I think this has to affect the way others look at her.

The really sad part about it all is that Kathy is a player the average golfer could easily relate to. She does not have a classic swing, but she gets the job done. She practices hard, particularly on her short game.

Kathy Whitworth, the LPGA's all-time leading money winner.

I mentioned a negative outlook. When Kathy hits a bad shot that's heading for trouble, she will often say, "Get in the bunker" or "Get behind that tree." She doesn't really want the ball in either place, of course, but it's a form of her negativism. The truth is that most of the other players would almost rather see Kathy in the middle of the fairway, because she is the world's greatest recovery artist. I don't mean just getting it up and down from the bunker, although she's peerless at that, too. Kathy has the gift of being able to create shots that extract her from jail.

Golfers of all levels can spend an interesting and useful day watching Kathy pop those little wedge shots out of heavy rough over a water hazard and stop them right at the flag. She's hooked and faded more balls around trees onto the green than any player I've seen. She hoods the face of her irons and punches the ball under a branch, or she lays back the face and floats the ball over the branch. She does it day after day, year after year. Nobody in our league can maneuver the ball like Kathy Whitworth.

At the same time, she has the reputation on tour of being a lucky player. Most of the gals claim Kathy gets more good lies in the rough and fewer bad lies in the bunkers than anyone. I wonder. What is it they say in the locker rooms of the football teams—that luck is the residue of hard work? Maybe if the rest of us had won over 75 tournaments and played the tour for 18 years we'd get a few more lucky breaks, too.

One thing about Kathy that amuses me is the way she can keep her hair in place. We can be playing on the most blustery day in the history of Palm Springs and Kathy will still look impeccable. Not a strand out of place. She ought to endorse and promote whatever hair spray she uses.

Judy Rankin really broke the barriers last year when she became the first woman golfer to earn $100,000 in one season. She deserved that honor, because Judy has been one of our best players for a long time. She has never been particularly colorful and she has a reputation of being an erratic putter, but for my money she's a magnificent player.

Judy is married to Walter S. (Yippy) Rankin, a gregarious, extroverted, shamelessly biased (in Judy's behalf) and altogether uninhibited man who travels with her on the tour. He follows her on every round, and he makes no attempt to stay out of the spotlight. You can hear him all over the course, exhorting Judy to greater effort and imploring that hanging putt to fall in.

On the practice tee in the mornings, when the girls discuss their pairings for the day, it's common to hear one say, "I've got Yippy." That means she has been paired with Judy and Yippy will be in the gallery. It's always an adventure.

In the 1976 Girl Talk Classic at New Rochelle, N.Y., Judy was among the leaders during the second round but could not get her putts to drop. She hit eight of the first nine greens and was two over par. On the way to the 10th tee, Yippy called Judy's caddie aside and suggested that maybe he wasn't reading the greens properly and that he had better shape up. Judy was stroking the ball too purely, Yippy insisted, to be missing all those putts. She had to be getting the wrong line.

A few years ago at Philadelphia, Yippy became so demonstrative and so distracting that Judy asked the marshals to remove him from the course. It was a gesture that most of us had been tempted to do ourselves on many occasions.

Until 1976 when Judy actually won $150,734 that season, she was not a good birdie putter. Isn't that a strange thing about golf? She could hole six-foot putts for pars by the hour, but get her over the same putt for a birdie and she could find all sorts of ways to miss. This is not

Talented Judy Rankin, who broke the $100,000-a-year barrier.

an unusual affliction among golfers—on the tour or in club events. The tendency is to bear down extra hard on a putt to avoid a bogey, but on a birdie putt it's easy enough to say, "Well, the worst I can make is par." Judy made a lot of birdie putts last season. Her stroke was smoother and more assured.

Judy is a spunky person, with a strong competitive drive. She is not a golfer you prefer to face down the stretch of a close finish, or in a playoff. She's tough. I think she is at her best in a 72-hole tournament because of her consistency, but her record in our normal 54-hole events is pretty darn good, too. Nobody else on the tour can play wind shots the way she can. Judy shot 68 in a typhoon during the final round of the 1976 Burdine's tournament at Miami, and she did the same thing three months later in the Dinah Shore when the gales were whipping the flags sideways. She won them both.

JoAnne Carner: Has any woman ever hit it farther?

Despite her unorthodox setup, I rate Judy the best striker of the ball on the tour. By unorthodox I mean her grip. Her left hand is turned clockwise so that it is virtually on top of the handle. Bob Toski tried to modify that, but Judy feels more comfortable with that grip and she went back to it. Who's to say what is the proper grip? Judy's grip works for Judy.

The great year that Judy had in 1976 speaks for itself. It's apparent that she needs a strong rudder like Yippy to guide her over the rough spots. Yet there are times when I think Yippy is too much the skipper, that his rein is too tight. Judy is an extremely intense woman, anxious to please her husband and her fans. Occasionally she puts extra pressure on herself to do it, and I'm sure it has hurt her game in the past. But she and Yippy make a good pair, and they've certainly added some needed color to the LPGA scene.

JoAnne Carner hits the ball about as far as any woman who ever lived. She drives it up to 270 yards, which makes it difficult to relate her swing to that of the average player. She has so much strength that she should be compared to a long-hitting man. She also is an excellent iron player and a steady putter. She won five U. S. Women's Amateur championships before joining the tour. In 1974, when she won six tournaments, she was named the LPGA Player of the Year.

As an amateur, JoAnne competed in many match play events. Match play is a different game than the one we play on the tour—it's a head-to-head contest. You don't have to worry about anyone else on the golf course except your opponent. As a result, your concentration and desire can become so strong they border on gamesmanship. In college we used to call it "psyching your opponent." I don't think JoAnne has ever quite made the total transition to stroke play.

While I admire the way she belts the ball, JoAnne is not an especially easy person to be paired with. She has an irritating habit of backing off from a putt. She will line it up, stand over the ball, then walk away from it. Her caddies claim it is merely a nervous habit, that she is not unsure of the line but merely uptight. That can become contagious. Watching her frittering around over a putt, I start getting jumpy myself.

JoAnne doesn't mingle much with the other women. She spends most of her hours off the course with her husband Don, who travels the tour regularly. Don Carner is no Yippy Rankin when it comes to theatrics, but I have noticed him biting his nails in the gallery.

There's no question in my mind that JoAnne Carner is the most exciting player on the women's tour to watch. Because of her great distance, she has a tremendous advantage over the field on par-5 holes and doglegs. She reaches more par-5s in two than anyone else, and by cutting the dogleg on par-4s with those big, high drives she is often left with just a wedge shot to the green. Her background in match play has infused her with a willingness to gamble. If JoAnne and I are in contention on the final round, I get nervous because she has the ability to make things happen.

One of the best examples I can think of occurred in the 1975 Ping Classic at the Camelback Country Club in Scottsdale, Ariz. Going into the final round I was two strokes behind JoAnne, who was leading. We were paired together, and I had the feeling we were in for a lively day of golf.

After getting birdies on four of the first five holes, I led by three strokes. I knew JoAnne was far from finished. She was pounding out those drives 30 to 50 yards in front of me, and hitting wedges to the greens where I was using 5-irons. By the 12th hole she had caught me. Then she faltered a little, and over the next three holes I picked up three strokes. I felt that three pars would win, but this was no time to change my style of play. What got me there was going to have to carry me home.

On the 16th, JoAnne recovered from a tee shot that nearly hooked out of bounds and hit a marvelous approach to the green. Then she holed a 20-foot putt for a birdie. I had to make a five-footer for my par. I looked over at JoAnne, who was watching me closely, and I said to myself, "You've just got to make this putt." I stroked it smoothly into the cup.

JoAnne had the honor on the 17th, a par-3, and hit the green. We were down to the basics of match play golf now. I knew I had to choke off her momentum somehow. I hit my tee shot inside of hers, but we both wound up with pars, and I was still leading by two on the final hole.

The 18th is a par-5 that JoAnne reached in two, and two putts later she had a birdie to cut my lead to one stroke. I needed par to win. The air was thick with tension, although it was very quiet out there in the desert. I managed to get my par and won by a stroke. But JoAnne had me scared to death.

I remember another instance, though, when JoAnne's full-throttle style of play backfired. It was on the final hole of the 1975 Babe Zaharias Classic in Cleveland. JoAnne and Judy Rankin, paired together behind me, were tied for the lead. I birdied the 17th hole and parred 18, which left me one stroke behind both of them. In trying to cut the dogleg on 18, JoAnne aimed her drive over some houses. It caught a tree and went out of bounds. Judy parred the hole and won the tournament; JoAnne's double bogey put her in third place.

Knowing JoAnne, she would probably take the same gamble again—and pull it off. She is some kind of player.

Sandra Palmer and I used to be close friends. She was my staunchest defender during my lawsuit problems with the LPGA and I'll always be grateful to her for that. In recent years we have drifted apart, seeking out other friends and other interests, although we respect each other's golf game. I still can look objectively at Sandra, the golfer, and I can tell you that she can be an ordeal to be paired with.

Golf did not come easy to Sandra. She spent seven years on the tour before winning her first tournament. It was a grind for her. In order to succeed, she developed the best short game on tour and she did it through hard work. Nobody on the tour spent more time practicing shots around the green. She would chip and putt for hours after each round. Golf was an obsession with her.

The compulsion to win became so strong that she developed an intensity that was distracting to her fellow players. During a round she would fidget with a practice swing while others were hitting. She would make quick, jittery little movements around the edge of the green while others were putting. I don't think Sandra realized what she was doing. She was all wrapped up in her own game, in her own world.

You've heard about some of the more competitive players on the men's tour—guys like Hale Irwin, Gary Player, Dave Hill. Sandra can match any of them. She comes to *play*. This makes her particularly ef-

Sandra Palmer, an icy competitor and old friend.

fective in four-ball competition. She loves these team events, and I speak from experience.

We teamed up twice to win the LPGA Four-Ball. In 1972 shortly after the LPGA tried to suspend me, we tore the tournament apart and won it by 10 strokes on a good course, New Seabury in Massachusetts. We had a 66 the final day and never had a bogey in the tournament. Sandra had improved her game sharply by acquiring a new set of shorter clubs. She is a short person who always had trouble getting her long iron shots into the air. The problem was that she was using men's clubs she could not handle. She went to a shorter, lighter set with women's flex in the shafts of both her woods and irons and the results were immediate. I could recommend the same technique for a lot of women who feel their clubs are too bulky.

In 1973 we returned to New Seabury for the Four-Ball and won it again. This one was more of a struggle. On the 15th tee of the final round we trailed the team of Sally Little and Jan Ferraris by two strokes. I felt my concentration had been wavering on the greens, so I stood over a 10-foot birdie putt for a second or two longer until I was sure of the line and rolled it in. On the 17th I did the same thing and made a downhill putt from 20 feet to give us a share of the lead.

We were paired with Sally and Jan, both good friends of mine. Things got tense when we reached the 18th green. Sally shook us up by holing a 25-foot birdie putt from just off the green. Then Sandra, that icy competitor, made her five-footer and off we went into extra holes. Sandra took care of that, too, by making a birdie putt of five feet on the first playoff hole.

In the last year or two, as Sandra became a consistent winner, I have noticed a change in her outlook. She seems less intense—more relaxed and more involved in things beyond the golf course. She is more popular with the other players on the tour. Sandra worked hard for what she has attained, and now she seems to be enjoying her golf and her life away from the course.

Donna Caponi was a fun-loving party girl when I turned professional in 1969. She was the Raymond Floyd of the women's tour. The girls called her the "Watusi Kid" because she loved to dance. She liked men, too. We used to kid her about getting cricks in her neck looking for men in her gallery.

Donna, Jan Ferraris and I took part in a golf driving exhibition in Busch Stadium one night during the week of a tournament at St. Louis. We met some of the Cardinal baseball players, and I went out after the game that night with one of them, George Culver. The next day George came out to the golf course, looking for me. He saw Donna first, and that was the last I ever saw of him.

Another pro athlete Donna dated was Roman Gabriel, who was then playing quarterback for the Los Angeles Rams. When Donna got married to Ken Young, she and Ken bought Gabriel's house near Los Angeles.

For all the social activity of Donna's early years on tour, she was an excellent player. She won the U.S. Women's Open back to back in 1969 and 1970, and was named Most Improved Woman Professional by Golf Digest in 1969.

A few years ago Donna went on a stringent diet to lose weight. The sudden change in body metabolism threw her timing off and she struggled through a couple of lean seasons. She came back to win two tournaments in 1975 and in 1976 she had a great year. Near the end of the 1976 season she won three straight tournaments—in Portland, Los Angeles and Japan.

Not only is Donna one of the toughest competitors on the tour, but she has a creamy tempo to her swing. She has the slowest backswing I've ever seen, something for all golfers to remember. She is a streaky

Donna Caponi Young, the Watusi Kid who became a golf star.

player, vulnerable to several weeks of bad golf; but when her putting is sharp, she can really string those good rounds together.

Of all the current players, I can't think of any who has made a greater contribution to the LPGA than Carol Mann. She was our president for two years during the mid-1970's, the time of our most rapid growth. Now she has become our spokesperson, the symbol of the new LPGA, with a warm and gracious personality that has charmed audiences at banquet speeches all over the country. She had the courage to lead the fight for a new commissioner in 1975 and she was instrumental in the hiring of Ray Volpe for that job. If you follow the women's professional tour at all, you know what a tremendous asset Ray Volpe has been for the LPGA.

At one time, early in her career, Carol was one of the longest hit-

We're all proud of Carol Mann and her contributions to the LPGA.

ters on the tour. Standing 6 feet 3 inches, she had a full, sweeping swing with a lovely arc. She has always been a student of the game, deeply involved in the mental aspects of golf, and she decided somewhere along the line to sacrifice distance for control. She learned to maneuver the ball beautifully, and with her natural putting stroke she has the ability to shoot low rounds on any course.

I have gotten to know Carol a little better in recent years, and I have nothing but the highest respect and admiration for her. She is, in every way, a credit to the LPGA and to women's sports.

Sandra Haynie plays slashing, aggressive golf and yet her outward appearance is just the opposite. She is incredibly phlegmatic. The expression on her face never seems to change, and walking off the 18th green you'd never guess whether she shot 69 or 79.

Fearless and phlegmatic, Sandra Haynie always "goes for it."

I don't know many golfers anywhere who attack the ball with more zest than Sandra Haynie. She'll go for anything, if there's one chance in 10 of making it. I wouldn't advise this approach for the average club golfer, but Sandra has the nerves and shots to pull it off. She's at her best on tough courses. Who could ever forget her finish in the 1974 U.S. Women's Open? She hit a 3-iron shot to the green on the 71st hole and made a 60-foot birdie putt. On the 72nd hole she got down a birdie putt from 10 feet. While the other leaders were tripping over themselves down the stretch, Sandra walked off with the championship.

It's hard to realize that Marlene Hagge has been playing the tour for over 25 years. She still has the glamour girl image. You can spot Marlene anywhere on the course, in trim, white slacks and a tight sweater or blouse.

Marlene Hagge, still a glamour girl after 27 years on the tour.

For a long time she had a curious habit of arriving at the course shortly before her starting time. If she were scheduled to tee off at noon, it was not surprising to see Marlene stroll in at 11:45 a.m., just in time to change her shoes and stroke a few putts. That amazed me. In recent years, with the arrival of so many good young players and the sharp increase in prize money, Marlene has been spending more time on the practice tee. We kid her a lot about that. It seems to me that Marlene's performance has improved correspondingly, which might be a good lesson to remember. Practice is essential, particularly in the competitive atmosphere of the tour, which is constantly being refueled with fresh talent.

Along with Kathy Whitworth and Carol Mann, Marlene is a deadly shotmaker from 50 yards in to the green. I think I know why those older players have such a great touch. When they broke in on the tour they

Jan Stephenson, the Australian eye-catcher who can really play.

were playing from men's tees on most courses. The holes played so long it was tough to reach the green in regulation figures, so the players had to learn finesse shots to survive.

Kathy, Marlene and Carol had been around a long time before Jan Stephenson first appeared in 1974. Jan came from Australia, where she had been not only a fine amateur golfer but also a journalist, to use that ennobling term for someone who writes about golf. She was cute, gifted with a quick mind and obviously loaded with ambition.

When I first saw Jan, I thought she was just another golfing glamour girl. I didn't think she had the game to hold up on the tour—or that she was willing to sacrifice her social life to get ahead. The guys were flocking after her, but Jan thought it was more important to work on her golf. One of her rituals, which she still continues, is to hit 100 putts from four feet every day. I couldn't take that strain on my back, and I doubt that many can. But Jan is a tough-fibered gal, physically and mentally.

Physical fitness is a mania with Jan. She pops down loads of vitamin pills, eats health foods and watches her diet carefully. You don't see her around the dining room at the hotels where we stay. She is more likely having dinner in her room, doing her exercises or practicing her putting stroke on the carpet.

Jan won her first LPGA tournament early in the 1976 season at Naples, Fla., by taking the lead early and then holding it down the stretch. She did not win the Colgate-Dinah Shore that April at Mission Hills, but she got a good deal of television exposure on the final day. Viewers saw a pert, lively woman with a good swing and a bright smile, a combination the public was looking for. She also did some TV commentary that week. When Jan stopped off in New York later in the season for an LPGA luncheon, Red Smith wrote a glowing column about her in The New York Times. Jan will go a long way.

Another of our 1974 rookies was Pat Bradley. I remembered Pat from my days in New Hampshire, although she is six years younger than I am. Pat is from Westford, Mass., just across the New Hampshire line. At the age of 14, she was competing in the New Hampshire Women's Amateur with a sound, all-around game. I worked with her on her short game a little that summer. A few years later, in the midst of my lawsuit hassle with the LPGA, Pat's mother called and offered me encouraging words of support. I've followed the progress of Pat Bradley rather closely ever since.

Pat joined the tour after finishing No. 1 in her qualifying school. She was a wild hitter with no lack of confidence. One of her first proclamations was that she was going to be the best golfer from New England on the tour. She was taking dead aim at my reign in that department.

After finishing second as Rookie of the Year in 1974, she improved her game considerably the next year when she won the Colgate Far East Championship. In 1976, she really came on and was honored by *Golf Digest* as the Most Improved Woman Professional.

Pat also made marked changes in her game. Instead of the old free-wheeling style of play, she became the essence of conservative golf. Pat often plays so conservatively that some of the girls call her "Lay-up Bradley." Maybe there's a lesson for all of us to learn here. Pat got to the point where she simply would not take chances on the course, and she began laying up whenever she had a chance. I've already mentioned earlier how she played short on the 72nd hole of the 1976 Carlton, a decision that I felt cost her an opportunity to finish second.

Earlier that season we found ourselves going head to head in a sudden-death playoff for first place at Wheeling, W. Va. That was on the

Pat Bradley, my new challenger as New England's best golfer.

Sunday in August when the fourth round of the men's PGA Championship at Washington, D.C. was washed out by rain. We were getting a
taste of the same storm over in Wheeling. Play was held up for more
than two hours in the afternoon, and it was well past dinner time when
Pat finished her final round as the leader on the board.

Coming into the final hole, I was one stroke behind. It was a par-5,
so naturally I cranked up and went for the green on my second shot. It
finished on the front edge, 100 feet from the pin. My first putt was six
feet long. Pat was there watching me as I looked over my second putt,
a nasty one with a left-to-right break. The green was still wet, which I
knew would reduce the break. I played it on the inside left edge of the
hole, accelerated my hands through the ball and stroked it in for a tie.

Since there was no television coverage that day, we went out to
the first hole for the playoff. Pat's swing was a little quick on the drive

and she hooked the shot. She also hooked her approach into a bunker. I hit a strong tee shot. Normally, I would have used a 6-iron for the second, but it was 7:30 at night, the air was heavy, so I went with a 5-iron. It finished on the green, 30 feet short of the pin.

Pat took three from the trap, missing her par putt from four feet. I thought she stroked it well, but it stayed out. My first putt came up only a couple of inches short of the cup. I tapped it in and I had my first victory of 1976.

I was elated, of course, but my euphoria was tempered by the realization that my status as New England's best woman golfer was going to be challenged often in the years to come. Pat Bradley will win her share.

Of all the rookies who have joined the tour since I first came on, I can't recall anyone who has received more publicity than Laura Baugh. Here she was, U.S. Women's Amateur champion, Curtis Cup player, blonde and beautiful. Moreover, she had signed with Mark McCormack. Shortly after signing with Mark, Laura made a reported $100,000 on a brief swing through Japan—even before she had hit her first shot on our tour.

There were two points of view about Laura early in her professional career. Some of our players resented all the money she was making. They felt that they had been out there beating balls for years, scratching out a living, and along comes this gorgeous doll who made all that endorsement money long before she proved she could win.

Jan Ferraris was originally one of them, and she was outspoken in her feelings. Gradually, Jan softened her outlook and almost without knowing it eased over in the other school of thought about Laura—that her commercialism was good for the tour. After all, she did attract the galleries and that's what we've always been looking for. Bigger galleries mean bigger purses. The more the girls considered that, the less they resented Laura.

One thing Laura had going for her was that she worked hard on her game. She never gave the impression that she was out just to capitalize on her looks. She spent hours on the practice tee. But I don't think she will win with her present swing.

The basic tenet of a good golf swing is the weight shift, in which you transfer the weight to your right side on the backswing and move it to your left side on the downswing as you come through the ball. I don't know of any other way to play golf.

But Laura doesn't swing that way. She has what is called the "reverse pivot." She sets up with the weight on the left side. At the top of her backswing, her weight is still on her left side. As she comes down through the ball, the weight transfers back to the right side. Jim Flick, the eminent golf instructor, wrote about this swing flaw in a recent magazine article. His description of the errors involved fit Laura like her tailored slacks.

Laura hits the ball straight, but not far; under pressure, her distance is reduced even further because the swing becomes more restricted. She had a chance to win the Wheeling tournament in 1976, the one in which Pat Bradley and I played off. Laura was tied for the lead on 15, a par-3, in the last round. She failed to make good contact with her tee shot and hit it well short of the green. It was a costly time for the reverse pivot to take its toll.

Whenever I pass up a tournament, I look for the scores in the morning paper. If I see that Laura has shot a good round, I can almost picture the course. Since she does not carry her approach shots a long way, she has trouble on a course with problems in front of the green. When she has a fairly high score, I know that the course was well trapped. When she's among the leaders, I know she was able to play the bump-and-run low shot, a technique she executes very well.

Time will tell about Laura, but I really think she ought to do something about her swing.

People are always asking me about Amy Alcott and Hollis Stacy, two of our better young players on the tour. I'll give you a capsule analysis. Amy has a super short game, and lots of confidence and poise. But she is not as good as she thinks she is. Hollis, on the other hand, is an under-rated player. She was a great golfer as a kid, winning three straight U.S. Junior Girls championships.

Hollis had to struggle and adjust on the tour like all of us, but she selected her instructors wisely—Jim Flick and Peter Kostis, who are among the best teachers in the country. We sometimes call her "Spacy Stacy" because she often appears to be in her own little world. Like the final hole at Sarasota in 1976, when she was tied for the lead. Everybody knew you had to hit something less than a driver on that hole because of a fairway water hazard, but Spacy hit one anyway and her ball sailed into the lake. She learned from that mistake, though, and I predict she will go on to enjoy a successful career on the tour.

Well, there it is . . . my "penetrating appraisal" of some of the cast of characters who make up the tour. They're quite a bunch. Life is never dull when you're going up against them week after week.

You can learn a great deal about golf from watching one of our tour events. Observe JoAnne Carner drive the ball or Judy Rankin hit those iron shots or Kathy Whitworth putt or Carol Mann work out of the bunker. They're the best in the business.

I remember an article Susie Maxwell wrote a few years ago for *Golf Digest*. It was entitled, "Watch Me, Not Arnie and Jack." What Susie meant was that men could learn more from watching the women pros rather than their male counterparts on tour, because their games relate more to ours. The men pros play an average par-4 with a driver and short iron. We play it with a driver and a 3-iron or 4-iron. Isn't that the way you have to play it?

Symbol of the tour's new image: vivacious and lovely Laura Baugh.

Susie had another point. Many of the men pros swing the club so fast it's just a blur. You *can* learn more about swing technique from watching the women. We work constantly on fundamentals, and our clubhead speed is not so great that you cannot see what we're doing.

The girls frequently work with each other, making swing checkpoints and offering constructive advice. Some people may consider this unusual, with all that money at stake. But that's the way the tour is. We are a little world of our own. There are always rivalries and petty jealousies, but we overcome them as we travel across the country, putting on our weekly show. It's a big step removed from the little caravan that Patty Berg and Babe Zaharias conceived 30 years ago.

5.

ON TRIAL

It was Saturday afternoon, May 20, 1972, the second round of the Women's Bluegrass Invitational at the Hunting Creek Country Club in Louisville. As I reached the 15th green, I was surprised to see Joyce Ann Jackson and Kathy McMullen, two tour players, in my gallery. It is very unusual for a golfer to go out on the course to watch someone else play. Eighteen holes of tournament golf leave you drained, physically and emotionally. But there they were, the two of them, and I remember thinking how nice it was of these girls to come out to see me play. I didn't know I was also being observed through binoculars from the television towers.

Up to that day it had been the happiest year of my life. I had won two tournaments, the Colgate-Dinah Shore and the Suzuki Internationale. I was the leading money winner on the tour, with just over $32,000. I loved being a professional golfer. I had many close friends, on the tour and all over the country. Life could hardly have been sweeter.

I didn't start out too well in the Louisville tournament, shooting 75 the first day and 40 on the front nine of the second round. But on the back nine I made five straight birdies, including one at the 17th hole where they were paying $500 for hitting it closest to the pin. I hit one in less than two feet away on 17. My score on the back nine was 32, which put me in position to pick up a nice check the next day.

Sandra Palmer and I had dinner that night at the Melrose Motel, and then we went to mass. After the service we were in Sandra's room watching television when the phone rang. It was 10:30 p.m.

The call was from Linda Craft, one of the five players then serving on the executive board of the LPGA. Linda apparently had been trying to reach me for several hours. "The executive board would like to see you," she said.

I had changed into my grubbiest clothes, shorts and a T-shirt. The last thing I wanted to do at that hour of the night was go to a meeting. "It's late, Linda," I said. "Can't it wait until tomorrow? Why do you want to see me now?"

"You'll find out."

So I went back to my room, changed clothes and went on down to Room 40 of the Melrose Motel for a meeting that would set off the two most tumultuous years of my life.

The entire executive board was there: Linda, Judy Rankin, Sharon Miller, Penny Zavichas and Cynthia Sullivan, president of the LPGA. Plus Marlene Hagge of the Tournament Committee and Gene McCauliff, who was then our tournament director and traveled the tour.

This was the center of power within the LPGA. We had an executive director, Bud Erickson, but he dealt mainly with sponsors. On a day-to-day basis the girls, with Gene's help, ran the show.

The atmosphere was frigid. Everyone looked very solemn. I was invited to sit down, so I sat on the bed. I still didn't know what was going on, but I could feel the room tingling with tension.

Without warning, they told me I had been observed moving my ball on the green that day, marking it incorrectly to my advantage. They said it wasn't the first time it had happened and that I was disqualified from the tournament right then and there. They said the official reason for the disqualification was that I had signed an incorrect scorecard.

"You're just the first in a movement," said McCauliff, who indicated that the organization was tightening up its rules and regulations. "Your eventual penalty may be severe."

By this time I was starting to panic. I was terribly hurt, and stunned. "Can't I defend myself?" I asked. "Isn't there anything I can do?"

McCauliff shook his head. "We had people out there watching you today. You mis-marked your ball. That's why you are being disqualified."

Gene McCauliff had sent Kathy McMullen and Joyce Ann Jackson out on the course to spy on me. Penny Zavichas said she had watched me through binoculars from the tower where she had been doing some television commentary for a Louisville station after she had finished her round. Penny claimed she had seen me move the ball forward on the 17th green. That's the hole where I hit it within two feet. I could have made that putt blindfolded.

I reminded Gene and the girls in the room that my playing partners that day, Lesley Holbert and Kathy Ahern, had signed my scorecard. Aside from the caddies and the marshals, they were the only other people inside the gallery ropes. McCauliff would later testify that he had spied on me earlier but never saw me do anything wrong.

It was now after midnight. The meeting was ready to break up. I glanced over at Sharon Miller, trying to catch her eye. We were close friends. That afternoon I had loaned her some tapes on putting called "Psych Up and Win." They were kind of a self-hypnosis thing, dealing with positive thinking. They had helped my putting. Sharon considered herself a mediocre putter and wanted help. I had taken the tapes to her room a few hours earlier and she thanked me for them. Why didn't she say anything to me then about this meeting?

After the girls dismissed me, I ran back to Sandra's room. "You're not going to believe what happened down there," I cried. "They threw me out of the tournament!"

The next day I watched from the gallery as Kathy Cornelius and Gloria Ehret tied for first place. Kathy won the sudden-death playoff. Nobody paid any attention to me. It wasn't that unusual for someone to be disqualified for signing an incorrect scorecard. The press had no inkling of the real reason. They had been told I had moved my marker one putter-width to get the marker out of the line of another player's putt, which is proper procedure, and had then forgotten to return my marker to the original spot.

At that time, nothing had been said about any fine or probation. That was to come the following week.

The next tournament was the Titleholders, held at the Pine Needles resort that Warren and Peggy Kirk Bell own in Southern Pines, N.C. On the drive to Southern Pines, Sandra and I stopped at Greensboro to see Ernie Vossler, Sandra's instructor. Ernie and his partner, a lawyer named John Russell, were building a golf course called the Cardinal.

Ernie had played the PGA tour before he got into the golf architecture business, and I trusted him. I told him the whole story about what happened at Louisville. "I'm not perfect," I said. "I may have marked my ball wrong at times. You know how difficult it is to put it back in the same spot every time. But I've never done anything intentionally wrong, and I can honestly tell you I've never tried to cheat."

I showed him how I prefer to mark the coin well behind the ball, so that if I'm nervous or tense under tournament pressure I would be sure not to touch it. Then I'd carefully return the ball to its previous position. It's something I had always done on the tour.

Ernie advised me to take that approach with the board at Pine Needles if they called me into another meeting. "Tell them you're sorry if you've done anything wrong," he said, "and promise them it will never happen again."

It wasn't the best advice I've ever received.

At Pine Needles I met with Cynthia Sullivan, Judy Rankin, Sharon Miller and Gene McCauliff. Penny Zachivas and Linda Craft were not there because they weren't eligible to play in that tournament.

Before we had a chance to really discuss the situation, they told me I had been put on probation and fined $500. I still didn't think the situation was all that serious. They asked me if there was anything I wanted to say. Remembering what Ernie had told me, I apologized for anything I had unintentionally done wrong and then added, "If all these things you say are true, I guess I've dug my own grave and I'll just have to live with it."

While the meeting was taking place in the dining room, several of the women, including Marlene Hagge and Louise Suggs, were sitting in the bar awaiting the news. Someone went right from the meeting to the bar and told them exactly what I had said. Shortly after, Jan Ferraris and Sally Little rushed up to me. "Janie," Jan said, "there's a lot of talk going on. They said you've admitted your guilt. They're talking now about suspending you."

After hearing this, I became desperate. I went up to Judy Rankin and asked her what was going on. She didn't say much. Neither did Cynthia. Marlene Hagge walked by and she gave me the most chilling, devastating look I've ever seen. I'll never forget that look.

Linda Craft   **Sharon Miller**

Betsy Rawls was there at the tournament. We all respected her. I went to her room and pleaded my case. I discovered I had been accused of moving the ball as much as two inches ahead of the marker. That was stupid, because I always had big galleries and there was no way I could get away with doing that during my two years on the tour. Betsy seemed to understand.

Then I heard some more rumors from Jan Ferraris. That night I went to see Sharon Miller, who was staying in a trailer park near the course, and I threw a tantrum. "Sharon," I screamed, "tell me what is going on! I thought you were my friend!"

I finally got Sharon to admit that I might be suspended. She said that I had cheated the LPGA and that by doing so I was taking money out of her pocket.

My next stop was Kathy Whitworth. I was trying to get some answers from people I respected. "Kathy," I said, "you know I don't

Cynthia Sullivan   **Penny Zavichas**

ever recall doing what they say. If I have ever mis-marked, it wasn't intentional and it certainly was minimal."

Kathy looked at me and replied, "Well, there's no such thing as being a little bit pregnant."

That week a petition urging my suspension for the balance of the 1972 season was circulated and signed by 29 players. The first signature on it was Marlene Hagge's. The petition contained the words, "In view of Jane Blalock's admission to the Executive Board that she had moved the ball . . . we, the undersigned members of the LPGA, demand that the Board take further action . . . and that she be suspended for the balance of 1972." The petition was never presented to any of my friends.

It was like mass panic. Nobody was thinking rationally. The girls were so wrapped up in this thing that none of them could play decent golf. Sandra Palmer won the Titleholders tournament by 10 strokes, with a 283 for four rounds. I shot 298 and tied for seventh.

On one of the rounds I was playing behind Sandra, who was paired with Marlene Hagge. The progression of play was slow. We were bunched together on the tee of a par-3 hole. Marlene accused me of telling Sandra what club I used on the previous shot. She didn't report her claim to Gene McCauliff, but she told the other girls that Sandra had asked what club I used and that I had told her. Sandra was furious.

After the round I walked up to the clubhouse and I could see groups of four or five girls talking. When I came by, there was total silence. I was getting the treatment.

After the tournament, Sandra and I drove back to Greensboro. I told Ernie the consequences of the approach he had suggested, and that I feared some drastic action was forthcoming. He got me on the phone to his partner, John Russell, whose law office was in New York. I told John the whole story.

John called Cynthia Sullivan and warned her not to take any further action until I had a full hearing with legal counsel—meaning with himself. He told me to proceed on to Baltimore for the next tournament, which was the Lady Carling Open.

I arrived in Baltimore on Tuesday night, May 30, in a pouring rain. There was a note at my motel to call Cynthia Sullivan immediately. She told me to come "at once" to the Hunt Valley Inn for a meeting. I called John Russell and he said that I should go, but he also reminded me that he had advised them not to take any action until he had a chance to represent me.

I got to the meeting, but the girls made me wait out in the hall for 30 minutes. When I finally got inside, they handed me their petition signed with 29 signatures and informed me that I was suspended for one year. It was like being hauled before a kangaroo court. I tried to argue with them, but it did no good. I remember my last words: "You are going to regret this decision."

Before dawn had broken the next morning I caught a flight to New York and landed at LaGuardia Airport at 7:45 a.m. I went straight to John Russell's office where several of John's partners joined us to assess the situation.

We realized that while the executive board had voted to suspend me, I actually had not yet been prevented from playing. The deadline for registration in the Lady Carling Open was 1:30 p.m. on Wednesday, just a few hours away. You don't have to register in person—a caddie can do it for you. As long as the entry fee is paid before the deadline, you're in the tournament.

My brother Jack was in Baltimore for the tournament. I had given him a check for my entry fee before leaving for New York. I reached him on the phone from John Russell's office. "Get out to the course right away," I told him, "and see if you can register me." He did, and when the lady at the registration desk saw the check, she immediately called for Gene McCauliff. McCauliff said the check could not be accepted, because Jane Blalock was not being allowed to play in the tournament.

As John pointed out to me, there it was—a clear violation of the Sherman Anti-Trust Act. Competitors were joining together to effect a group boycott and deprive me of my legal right to engage in interstate commerce, which the tour was. We had grounds for a lawsuit.

The Sherman Anti-Trust Act involves the regulation of trade by monopolistic tactics. It has been held since 1914 to "prevent collective refusals to deal, or group boycotts, as illegal *per se.*"

Consider these examples: Say that the New England Patriots and the Baltimore Colts got together and said, "We don't want to play the New York Jets. We don't like the locker room facilities they provide." Or Dave Cowens of the Boston Celtics makes an agreement with Walt Frazier of the New York Knicks not to play New Orleans because they contend that Pete Maravich steps over the line on his free throws. You just can't do these things.

We decided to sue for $5 million—$1 million for violation of the anti-trust law, to be trebled, plus $1 million in compensatory damages and another $1 million in punitive damages. That figure was selected as insurance against the possibility that the suspension might stand, and that legal delays would keep me from competing on the tour for an even longer period of time. Few professional athletes ever return to top form following an extended absence. If I should be kept out for any lengthy period of time, and then win the lawsuit, my lawyers felt I should be amply compensated.

The decision was made to file the lawsuit in Atlanta, because it was then the home office of the LPGA. We prepared a brief that sought a temporary injunction against the suspension. I returned that night to Baltimore, with plans to meet with John and two of his associates, Jerry Olshinsky and Larry Kill, two days later in Atlanta.

We went into court with our application for a temporary injunction before Judge Charles A. Moye, who was to become a very important man in my life. He studied the brief and granted the restraining order that same day, June 1. It was to be in effect for 10 days, which meant I could play in the next tournament, the LPGA Championship at Pleasant Valley Country Club in Sutton, Mass. Any prize money I won in that tournament would be held in escrow until further court action.

I spent the next few days with my family in Portsmouth, then drove down to Boston to meet Sandra Palmer's plane. Sandra was the staunchest friend I had left. On the drive to Pleasant Valley, she described how the LPGA was probing into my past, trying to dig up some dirt. They found out I had gone to a lot of beer parties while attending Rollins College, and that I had been put on probation there for staying out all night. That was true enough, but I'd heard a rumor was circulating that while on the tour I stood up on the bar in some tavern one night and took off all my clothes. That was clearly false.

Leaving the Atlanta courtroom with my attorney, John Russell, in June, 1972, after obtaining an injunction which allowed me to

continue to play. Behind us are lawyers Larry Olshinsky (left) and
Gene Partain, and my good friend LeaLea Brown.

My practice round partners that Tuesday were Sandra, Ruth Jessen and Joyce Kazmierski. Spectators were peering at me from all over, like I was some sort of circus freak. The ninth green, near the clubhouse, is elevated. Walking up the hill, I saw a battalion of people waiting behind the green. It was the press. They pulled and tugged at me, shoving microphones into my face. It was unbelievable. The interviews lasted so long I could play no more golf that day.

I was staying at the Pleasant Valley Motor Lodge, the tournament headquarters. The next morning when I walked into the coffee shop for breakfast, it was like entering a refrigerator. Instead of the usual chatter, there was an eerie silence. People even turned their backs as I walked by. I was supposed to play a practice round that day with DeDe Owens, but she called and said she didn't dare play with me. She was afraid of being ostracized by the other girls.

It is my belief that the two women largely responsible for my suspension were Marlene Hagge and Louise Suggs. This was difficult for me to understand, because they were both veterans and respected members of the LPGA, women I had idolized earlier in my career. I remember being paired with Louise Suggs in the fourth tournament of my rookie year (which, ironically, was also at Pleasant Valley). I thought it was such an honor. Louise was one of the founders of the LPGA, a great champion who had won 50 tour victories and was already installed in the LPGA Hall of Fame.

Three years later, Louise signed an affidavit accusing me of mismarking my ball that day at Pleasant Valley. The document was never used in court.

In 1971 I encountered another incident involving Louise Suggs. I had just moved down to Boca Raton, and I wanted to join a nice golf club where I could pay my own way and have a quality place to practice and play. LeaLea Brown and Norma Shook, two close friends, took me over to the Pine Tree Golf Club in Delray Beach. A big portrait of Louise Suggs hung in the women's locker room. She was considered Miss Pine Tree. I went before the board to apply for membership, was accepted and paid my $2,000 initiation fee.

It was about that time that I started playing golf in shorts, which became my trademark, along with the pigtails. I wore them all the time in tournaments, weather permitting. Well, after playing for a brief time at Pine Tree in shorts, I was called into the manager's office. He said some of the women had complained about my attire, and the club had passed a rule prohibiting shorts on the course. He asked why I couldn't play in a skirt. "I don't even have a skirt," I told him. "Shorts are my image." He said I couldn't wear them anymore at Pine Tree.

So I resigned my membership, and the story that appeared in the papers about the incident made Pine Tree look very stuffy. Louise took offense and wouldn't speak to me. Later, she confided to LeaLea Brown how angry she was with me for making Pine Tree appear such a stodgy club.

In 1972 Louise wasn't even playing the tour regularly anymore, but here she was involved in instigating my suspension. I believe it all went back to that Pine Tree incident.

Meanwhile, the harassment at the Pleasant Valley tournament continued. It was a strange situation, because Sutton is located near my home area, and a lot of my friends came down for the tournament. They helped counter-balance the flak I was getting from the other tour players.

My parents came also. We were having breakfast on the Thursday morning of the first round—it was a 72-hole event—when my mother spotted Debbie Austin's mother across the room. She and my mother had been close friends ever since Debbie and I were at Rollins together. Mom, who was really angry at the treatment I was getting, has a streak of Irish in her, so she got up and walked across the coffee shop to say hello to Debbie's mother. At the next table were Marlene Hagge and Judy Rankin. Debbie's mother was so upset by Mom's greeting that she spilled her coffee. It was kind of funny at the time, but three months later the whole thing, and other incidents like that, finally got to my mother. She wound up in the hospital with a bleeding ulcer.

Throughout the tournament that week, I was followed constantly on the course by other players who had finished earlier. When I was lining up a putt, they would stand around staring at me. It was as if they were trying to haunt me. Jan Ferraris told them they were handling it all wrong. "The more you hassle and heckle her," Jan said, "the better Janie will play. That's the way she is. She's a fighter."

That same week some comments by Bob Toski broke on the wire services. Interviewed on the phone by a writer in Miami, Toski was quoted as saying that I was a very intense competitor with a compulsive desire to win. It was inferred that if the charges against me were true, I might need some psychiatric help. When my mom saw the story in a Boston paper, she hid it from me so I couldn't read it. Dad got on the phone with Toski and said some unkind things to him. Bob denied the accuracy of the story, saying that he was quoted out of context and that several facts had been distorted.

I called him a week later and was satisfied that the article had not appeared the way Toski intended. Later on, in December, he provided a favorable deposition for our case in the event we would need it for a trial. Bob and I are still good friends. And I agree, by the way, with one observation he made: I do have a compulsive desire to win. The day I lose that desire is the day I get off the tour.

With all that going on, it's remarkable that I played as well as I did in the LPGA Championship. On a tough course, in rainy and cold weather, I shot 74–75–76–74 for 299 and second place. I was in contention all the way until the last few holes. Kathy Ahern shot a tremendous final round, a 69 with six birdies, to beat me by six strokes.

I remember the last round so well. I was paired with Sharon Miller and Kathy Whitworth. I had played with Sharon on Saturday, too, and

Marlene Hagge   **Louise Suggs**

she had been relatively friendly. But on the final day she was as cold as Kathy. Whenever either one of them would hit a good shot, the other would shout encouragement. But when I hit one, they said nothing.

At the presentation ceremonies, nobody said a word to me all during the program. The girls were obviously upset that I had played so well, but the gallery gave me a big hand—just as they had done all week. Later, Marlene Hagge went over to my mother and said she was sorry for all that had happened. I thought that was pretty strange, since I felt it was Marlene who had created so much of the trouble in the first place.

We were scheduled to play the Heritage Village Classic the next week at Southbury, Conn. Legally, I wasn't sure about my status. Once the 10-day temporary injunction was up, I had to get a permanent injunction before I was allowed to play. But it rained so hard that week, there was considerable doubt about whether the tournament would be played at all. Finally, it was just washed out. I spent long hours in my room at the Harrison Inn, watching the rain pour down and wondering what my future would hold. It is a sickening and helpless feeling, knowing that your life is in the hands of others. Worse still, I had no battlefield that week to unleash my frustrations.

Rumors were flying that the LPGA had movies of me illegally marking the ball on the green, which turned out to be false. There was another story that they had a deposition from a man in Kansas City who saw me move my ball the entire length of a club in the rough. That happened to be a tournament in which we had to play the ball "up" because of the weather and *everyone* was allowed to move the ball a club length. There was no end to these stories, and from everything I heard the girls were certain my suspension would be upheld.

The bombshell dropped the following week, on the Wednesday before the U.S. Women's Open at the Winged Foot Golf Club in Mamaroneck, N.Y. Judge Moye granted me a permanent injunction against the suspension. That was the single most important legal development of the entire ordeal. I was entitled to continue playing golf. The money I earned was to be held in escrow by the courts for an indefinite time.

Informed of the decision by Lincoln Werden of The New York Times, I ran screaming off the clubhouse patio and grabbed my brother Jack. We spun each other around joyously. Then I rushed into a phone booth to call my lawyers. The booth was surrounded by reporters, all waiting to talk to me. It was my happiest day in more than a month.

In his written order, Judge Moye declared: "The court finds, on the basis of the record before it, that the factors weigh clearly and heavily in favor of the granting of the injunction . . . . With respect to the probability or ultimate success or failure of the suit, the court again finds, on balance, that this factor weighs heavily in plaintiff's favor."

He was referring to the aspects of the Sherman Anti-Trust Act and the tactic of fellow competitors joining together to create an illegal boycott.

The judge also pointed out (referring to the affidavit of Linda Craft, which contained my comment, "I've dug my own grave and I guess I'll have to live with it") that "Plaintiff vigorously disputes the preciseness of the above language and claims that on the occasion in question, her response was a conditional one and that she informed the LPGA that any infraction of the rules was purely unintentional on her part." The order concluded with the declaration that . . . "It has not been necessary for the court to consider any matters relating to the question of whether or not plaintiff actually committed the violations of which she was accused, or whether, assuming that she did, the actions of the executive board of the LPGA in imposing its sanctions were proper."

With my future prize money held up by the courts, we had to post a $15,000 bond, which my father managed to do by putting up some old stock he had. The court actually held my money for only a few weeks, and eventually I began receiving government checks from the court for the amount of prize money I had coming.

Needless to say, the LPGA was not happy with the decision. I especially remember Marlene Hagge's comment: "Obviously, the judge is not a golfer." Actually, Judge Moye is.

The LPGA appealed the decision to the Fifth Circuit Court in New Orleans, which decided at the time not to rule on it. John Russell later told me the LPGA had filed its appeal after the deadline.

I should say something here about my relationship during this time with Bud Erickson, the LPGA executive director. Actually, there was no relationship. He never spoke a word to me. He never said, "I don't like you" or "You're hurting the LPGA" or anything. I felt he handled the whole incident in a chicken-like manner, like he was hoping the problem would go away or miraculously solve itself.

Despite Judge Moye's decision, my ordeal was a long way from over. I commuted in and out of Atlanta a total of 20 times for depositions and affidavits. One side would file a motion and the other would file a cross-motion. I was in touch constantly with my attorneys. I had to pay all my expenses, and my legal bills were piling up. But that was nothing compared to the harassment I continued to encounter on the tour.

What really bugged me was that several of the girls had claimed I had been mis-marking balls for a couple of years. They brought up a tournament at Alamo, Calif., in 1971, and in Atlanta that same year. If this was true, why didn't somebody say something to me at the time? My scorecards had all been signed by my playing partners. The LPGA even questioned my caddies, who swore they saw nothing irregular in the way I marked my ball. JoAnne Carner and I had been playing $1 matches for several years, all on a friendly basis, by matching cards at the end of our rounds. She never had a word of complaint. Suddenly she stopped speaking to me, and claimed she would refuse to play if she were paired with me again. That threat never materialized.

Things got hot in the George Washington Classic, near Philadelphia, which was held the week following the Women's Open. That's where Sandra Palmer got into trouble with the LPGA for supporting me.

Sandra was coming out with some pretty strong comments in the papers. One of them declared, "If you see an infraction, you point it out immediately. You don't wait until three years later to bring up something. Once you've signed the card, you're as guilty as the person who committed the infraction."

That was mild compared to this statement: "One of the girls signed an affidavit against Jane Blalock and I know she lied." Sandra was referring to Marlene Hagge, who thereupon sued Sandra for slander. Placed on probation for her comments, Sandra sued the LPGA. At the same time, the LPGA had filed a counter-claim against me, in an attempt to strip me of the prize money I had won while I was allegedly

Sandra Palmer facing an inquisition from the press. During the lawsuit she was never reluctant to give an opinion.

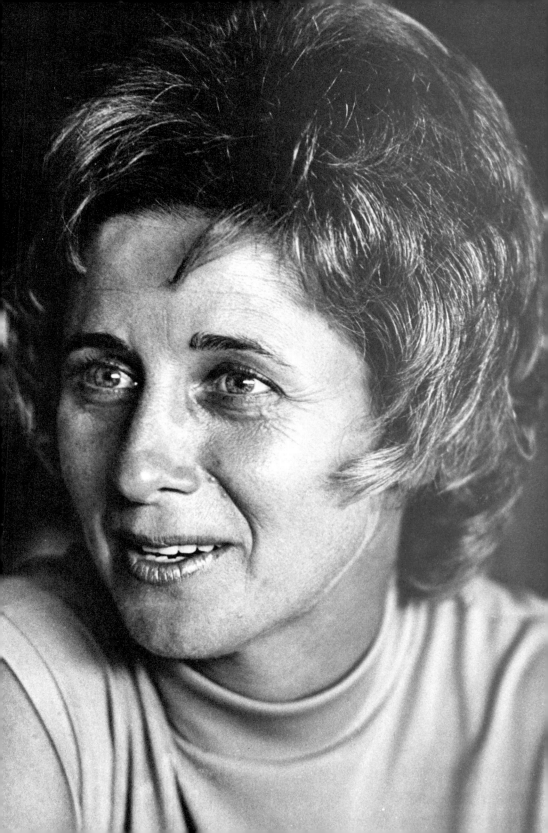

cheating. It was like a hair-pulling contest. Sandra's probation was lifted after a few months, however, and she dropped her lawsuit against the LPGA. Marlene also dropped her slander suit against Sandra. Nothing ever came out of the LPGA's counter-claim against me. But the atmosphere on the tour was rife with tension and hard feelings.

My mail really piled up during the Philadelphia tournament. When one of the people in the pro shop asked Gene McCauliff what he should do with it, Gene replied, "Tear it up and throw it away for all I care." Gene later claimed he made the remark in jest.

Animosities were flaring everywhere. I had won the tournament the year before, and I had a good following among the fans in the Philadelphia area. On the first tee for the opening round, they gave me a great hand and I could hear a lot of comments like, "Go get 'em, tiger" and "Show those broads who can play golf." It only antagonized the other girls all the more.

One of the most unpleasant episodes took place during the second round. I was paired with Judy Rankin and Judy Kimball. Neither one spoke a word to me during the whole round. Four hours is a long time to spend under those conditions, and it was a terribly depressing experience.

For the first time since the meeting in Louisville, my golf game began to deteriorate. The tension had affected my concentration to the extent that I could hardly swing the club back. I had a headache that lasted for days. I was playing scared on every shot.

Sandra Palmer kept speaking out in my behalf, and the girls were really giving it to her. Cynthia Sullivan called a press conference and accused the writers of being one-sided toward me. I must say that the press did treat me favorably throughout the whole ordeal. Cynthia didn't like that, and she criticized the writers.

The situation reached the point where the tournament committee sent out a National Guard escort to accompany me on the course during the last two rounds. Nobody ever explained whether the men were assigned to protect me from harm or harassment, or merely to allow my threesome to keep up with the pace of play. I had especially big galleries that week.

Our next stop on the tour was Angelo's Four-Ball tournament at New Seabury, Mass. Sandra Palmer and I scored a decisive victory there by playing 54 holes without a bogey on the card. Two weeks later, I was off to Atlanta.

I had won the Atlanta tournament the two previous years. The program for the 1972 tournament had two pictures of me on the cover, almost like a double image, denoting my back-to-back wins there. Inside the program was a large fold-out picture of me. I heard that several of the girls got together in a motel room one night and used the fold-out picture as a dart board.

In Dallas at the Civitan Open, circumstances became so bad they

Holing the putt to beat Kathy Whitworth in the 1972 Dallas playoff . . .

were almost ridiculous. But at least I had the satisfaction of winning that tournament, my first victory in a regular tournament since the LPGA mess started. I played steady golf throughout the week, and after holing out on 18 in the last round, I was leading. Kathy Whitworth needed a birdie on the final hole to tie me. Kathy is a great competitor, and she hit an iron shot just two feet from the hole. The girls who had gathered around the green were screaming and yelling with joy, and some of them grabbed the public address microphone to shout encouragement to her. Kathy made the putt, and we went into a sudden-death playoff on the first hole.

We drew straws for the honor and Kathy won. This prompted another cheer, and when she hit a good drive it set off more yelling. I hit my drive off to the right behind some trees and the girls were cheering that, too.

As I was lining up my second shot—a 5-iron that I had to fade around the trees—I noticed about 10 of the girls standing right behind the gallery rope, just five feet away from me. It was obvious they were trying to upset me. I hit a good shot and then Kathy laid up near a bunker, about 40 yards short of the green. Her third shot was on the green, 30 feet from the hole, and they even cheered that. I hit mine 10 feet past the hole. Kathy putted first, lagging it up six inches away, and then tapped it in for her par. Now I had a chance to win by making that 10-foot putt.

The caddie I had that week was a big black man named Jesse. They called him "Cryin' Jesse." He called me "Bula." I asked him one day what that meant and he said, "It means tough player." Now he looked over that downhiller and said, "Bula, we've got to make this putt." I rolled it in, and in my exhilaration I threw the putter about five feet in the air. The girls turned away and walked back glumly to the clubhouse.

The next week at Waco, while I was on the practice green, Gene McCauliff informed me I had to pay a $50 fine. I thought he was kidding. I laughed and said, "What have I done now?"

"You threw your putter in Dallas."

There's an automatic $50 fine in our bylaws for throwing a club, so I paid up. But it was worth it.

One of the most memorable newspaper clippings came out of that Dallas tournament. The headline read: "Blalock Dumps Establishment." Someone had the headline engraved onto a plaque for me and I've treasured it ever since.

The Civitan had been conducted in an atmosphere of bitterness and hostility. I'd contributed to that. Both sides had agreed not to fight the battle in the press, in a sort of mandate against public pronouncements. I'm afraid I violated that agreement in Dallas, even though my lawyers had warned me not to make any provocative statements. A writer named Harless Wade called me one night and repeated some of the things Kathy Whitworth had said earlier. He was looking for an

. . . and throwing the putter in glee, which cost me a $50 fine.

angle, because Kathy lived in Dallas and was very popular there. I got mad and said some things I shouldn't have said, things that came out later in a court hearing and in depositions. The paper carried the story under a "Blalock Asserts Not Guilty" headline. Kathy was really angry with me, and my attorneys weren't too happy about it, either. Some of the other girls called me up that night at Sandra's house and ripped into me for violating the agreement. I have to admit I was wrong in that case.

All in all, it was a very tense week. And then to have it end the way it did, with Kathy and me in a sudden-death playoff . . . . Well, all I can say is that it was a very satisfying thing to beat Kathy in her home town in front of a hostile gallery.

My relationship with most of the girls on the tour kept deteriorating. Those who were my true friends, like Sandra Palmer, Jan Ferraris, Ruth Jessen and Sally Little, were all the closer because of the trouble. But there was a real gulf between myself and some others.

The annual LPGA Players Meeting of 1972 was held during the Lincoln-Mercury Open at the Round Hill Country Club in Alamo, Calif., during the last week of September. It was always a big deal, with everyone expected to attend. I walked into the room and sat down like everybody else. Cynthia Sullivan got up and said, "Janie, you are not a member in good standing of the LPGA. You are now being asked to leave."

"I'd like to stay."

"You must leave the room."

So I did, but I felt I was entitled to stay, since technically I was not suspended.

A few weeks later, in the Portland Open, I noticed one of the tournament marshals moving inside the ropes to watch me very closely on the greens. He apologized, saying that the executive board of the LPGA had told him to spy on me.

The entire two years between the suspension and the final trial became a living hell for me. I cried myself to sleep most of the time. My religion is Catholicism. Although I was referred to once in a magazine article as a "casual Catholic," I do have my own strong religious beliefs. I would put my rosary beads in my hand each night when I went to bed. Within a short time they were all cracked and broken.

I hated to get up in the morning. I dreaded each new day, knowing what it would be like on the golf course and around the clubhouse. I was always overhearing little remarks made by groups of girls. There would be portions of articles or poems tacked up on the locker room bulletin board, just random pieces that might contain the words "honor" or "cheating." These words would be underlined, and my named scrawled across the sheet.

My nervous system took a real beating. I had always talked rather rapidly, but now my speech became non-stop. My hands would shake uncontrollably whenever I read the newspaper. My hair was falling out. I would reach up and pull out a fistful. Occasionally, I'd look at myself in the mirror and ask, "How much more of this can you take?"

When I visited my parents at home, I hardly spoke a word. I was totally withdrawn. My mother had a hard time coping with this. She says now that I wasn't the same person during those two years, that she scarcely recognized me. I really couldn't share this ordeal with my parents. I had to do that with my friends. Norma Shook and LeaLea Brown, who were involved in the Pine Tree incident, were bastions of strength. So was Freda Kant, a friend from Dallas who took care of Sandra's house. Sandra was great, too. They were the greatest friends anybody could have.

I tried to keep fighting. I sought out every resource I could find to help me endure. For about a year, I was sustained by my competitive instincts. I felt that by beating the other girls on the course I was vindicating myself. I know that nothing will ever faze me again, and that I will be able to overcome any emotional experience as long as I live.

On the tour I tried to stay away from the other girls as much as possible. I selected motels away from tournament headquarters. The locker room atmosphere was so bad I changed into golf shoes in my car. I never left my golf clubs around where anybody could get at them. Right after the round I would lock them in the trunk of my car, and at night I would carry the bag into my room.

Sandra and I would play our practice rounds together early in the morning, before most of the others had arrived at the course, or late in the afternoon after they had finished. Every day of every week there were interviews. Whether I shot 68 or 82, I'd be called into the press room afterward. I swear I've had more interviews than Muhammad Ali.

My galleries had always been large, but now they were multiplied by curiosity seekers. They were watching me to see if I really did cheat. One day at Columbus I was paired with Betty Burfeindt. My ball was already on the green when Betty had a shot from the fairway. Her ball struck mine and knocked it back about six feet. The procedure then is to confer with your playing partner to determine where your ball had been originally, then move it back to its original spot. This is in the USGA Rules of Golf.

Well, that's what I did, and then I heard someone in the gallery cry, "My gosh, she really does do it!"

It occurred to me that, through it all, I was making some new friends. I was losing a lot of old ones, but maybe it was a good way to weed them out.

I've brought out many of these things because there was no way during this time that I could either prove my innocence or disprove my guilt. It was like a swearing contest. I said I didn't; they said I did. Not even the final trial, in August of 1974, resolved that. The trial was based solely on the anti-trust aspects. Even if I had committed flagrant violations of the rules, the way the case was structured I still would have won the lawsuit.

At the same time, the tension was wearing on my nervous system. Your nerves can take only so much, and then they begin to burn out. We'll have to wait and see just how much of a long-range effect this experience had on my career, but I know it eroded my game for more than two years and set my development back as a professional golfer. I played the best golf of my life in 1976, but I have to think I could have reached that level in 1972 and 1973 under normal conditions.

After leading the tour in money winnings for much of the 1972 season, I finished second with a total of $57,323 to Kathy Whitworth's $65,063. In 1973, when my nervous system was taking such a beating, I slipped to ninth with $40,711. I came back with a good season in 1974, finishing second in money winnings with $86,442 and led the tour that year in performance average. In 1975, when I should have been able to concentrate better with the lawsuit over, I slipped back again to sixth place with $45,478. I have to attribute that to an overall letdown.

There were two incidents that boosted my morale. Lenny Wirtz had been our executive director when I first joined the tour. He was a tough, bouncy little guy, who refereed college basketball in the off-season. Nobody thought for a long time to ask him about my conduct. Finally someone did. Lennie replied, "Janie did nothing irregular that I know of. If I had thought she did, I would have grabbed her by the pigtails and slapped her ass."

One day at the Orange Blossom Classic in St. Petersburg, I was told that George Zaharias, Babe's husband, wanted to meet me. He was in a wheelchair. He shook my hand and said, "I just felt like saying hello. You're a gutsy woman. Babe would have admired you."

6.

FIGHTING BACK

Now that it's all over, there is still a residue of bitterness. I'll have a hard time ever again being on friendly terms with some of the girls. The wounds are too deep. Cynthia Sullivan, Penny Zavichas and Linda Craft are off the tour now, so I don't even think about them. Sharon Miller still doesn't speak to me, but I can get along without her friendship.

Judy Rankin and I go about our business with no problems. I was happy to see her have such a great year in 1976. There is a certain coolness between myself and both JoAnne Carner and Kathy Whitworth. I suppose it will be erased with the passage of time. Louise Suggs has tried to be friendly with me, but I've made it clear that I don't want to have anything more to do with her. Marlene Hagge and I have somewhat buried the hatchet. We've served on several committees together, including one in 1974 when we campaigned with the USGA to have the prize money increased for the Women's Open.

Some of the girls who really stuck by me, in addition to Sandra Palmer and Jan Ferraris, are Sandra Haynie, Sally Little, Mary Bea Porter and Ruth Jessen. Ruthie has been super. There's also Sybil Griffin, who was playing the tour with Marlene, Mickey, Louise and the others back in the late 1950's and early 1960's. Sybil has been a staunch ally. She's a teaching professional now in Delray Beach, not far from my home, and I see her frequently. She comes out to watch all the tour events in Florida and has gone out of her way to be gracious to me. For awhile some of the older girls wouldn't speak to Sybil because of this. She told me, "Don't worry about that. I can handle it. If that's the way they want to be, let them."

Even with this support, I was a pretty bleak and desolate person late in 1972. At times I felt as though my nerves were wound so tight they would snap at any minute. I developed a temporary cure: whenever the jitters hit me on the course, I'd put myself into a kind of hypnotic trance and just stare at the water or the trees. It was a lonely existence.

Fortunately, the "Year of the Lawsuit" wound up on a happy note. Our last tournament of 1972 was the Lady Errol Classic, played at Errol Estate Country Club in Apopka, Fla., just outside Orlando. It was like a homecoming for me, since Rollins College is located in that area and I had many friends there for the tournament. My two brothers, Jack and Jim, were also on hand.

Jim, who had never seen me win a tournament, had a rabbit's foot that his girl friend had given him. He carried it in his pocket throughout the tournament. I was still in contention but needed birdies on the last

Monsignor James Kelley with a grateful friend.

two holes to get into a playoff with Kathy Whitworth and Sandra Palmer. On the 17th hole of the final round, Jim came up to me and said, "Give me your putter." He took out his rabbit's foot and then rubbed my putter with it. I immediately sank a long birdie putt of 20 feet, followed by another one of eight feet on 18.

You can imagine the emotions involved in that playoff. Sandra Palmer, who had been sticking her neck out for me for months, and Kathy Whitworth, who was still chafing from our playoff at Dallas several weeks earlier, and I were all gathered at the first hole for the sudden death. Someone in the gallery shouted, "I don't want Blalock to win, she's a cheat." My brother Jim yelled right back, "She's not a cheat, she's my sister."

Just a nice, friendly atmosphere to get the thing under way.

We all parred the first two holes. On the third hole, a par-3 over water, I hit a 6-iron about 20 feet from the pin and made my birdie putt.

It was a great way to close out an abrasive season.

That winter, while playing an exhibition at Fort Lauderdale, Fla., I was introduced to a Catholic priest named Monsignor James Kelley of Ridgewood, N.J. I found him a very comforting man to be with. He invited me to see him again at St. Croix, in the Virgin Islands. Monsignor Kelley urged me to unburden the whole thing from my mind. We celebrated mass every morning for a week, then talked in the afternoon. For the first time I was able to unleash all my feelings — and I also learned a good deal of what my religion was all about.

Monsignor Kelley even arranged for me to have an audience in Rome the next winter with Pope Paul VI. I wasn't sure I should go. It was during January, right in the midst of my practice schedule for the upcoming tour season. I asked Tom Nieporte, my golf instructor and a good friend, what I should do.

"You've got to go, Janie," Tom said. "A trip like that will help you so much in the long run. Later on, if things go against you, I want you to think of the meeting you'll have with the Pope and you'll gain strength from it."

So my mom and I went over to Rome and had our audience with the Pope. It was brief. He spoke very broken English, but I remember him telling me to have faith and confidence. I guess it's about the closest I'll get to heaven in this life.

But I'm getting a little ahead of my story. I saw the Pope in January of 1974. After my week with Monsignor Kelley late in 1972, I still had the 1973 season to face, and it was not a particularly pleasant one.

I had sustained myself through the last part of 1972 mostly on resolve and a desire for revenge. But by 1973 the fight had been drained out of me. The only tournament I won was the Four-Ball with Sandra Palmer. I finished ninth on the money-winning list. And there were more nasty incidents.

One of them was initiated at the Sears Classic at Port St. Lucie early in the season. A magazine writer approached me and asked if I would participate in a television program to benefit cancer research in West Palm Beach. I said I would, but when I showed up for the program, I was told it had been "cancelled."

The same man asked me to donate something to be auctioned off later at a fund-raising event for cancer. I sent him a set of my wood club covers, but it was inadvertently mailed to the wrong address. The man wrote a nasty piece about my irresponsibility and suggested that perhaps the LPGA was right in going after me. It seemed I couldn't win no matter what I tried to do.

In the 1973 Colgate-Dinah Shore tournament at Mission Hills, which had been expanded to 72 holes and a purse of $135,000, I was involved in a weird ruling. Kathy Whitworth and I were both penalized, so I can't really claim any individual discrimination, but it was a situation that I believe resulted from all the lawsuit tension and could easily have been avoided.

It occurred during the second round on the sixth hole, which has two water hazards. I was playing with Kathy and Carol Mann. Kathy and I each hit a shot into the water. Kathy took a drop and then hit her next shot onto the green. Suddenly the gallery was buzzing. Something was wrong, but I didn't understand what it was. So I dropped a ball over my shoulder and hit over the green. Kathy walked over to me and said, "I think we both made an illegal drop. This is a direct hazard, not a lateral hazard." We asked for a ruling and were told that the infraction would cost us each two strokes. I remember thinking Kathy could have brought it up *before* I made my shot.

After the round, in which I shot a 73 for a sixth place tie, I felt like I was undergoing what they call "cruel and unusual punishment." I might have been treated more kindly if I had committed murder. It was like a sledgehammer that kept pounding me over the head. I remember walking off the 18th green that day and asking myself, "Is this ever going to end?"

During this time, my lawyers were getting the definite impression that Judge Moye wished to have the case settled out of court, that he felt the LPGA could not win and wished to avoid having the organization dragged through needless expense. The judge questioned why my punishment was increased from disqualification to probation and from fine to suspension, all for allegedly committing the same offense.

We obtained a deposition from Bob Toski, thanks to some efficient work by John Russell, who flew down to Miami and met with Toski the day before he left on a trip to Japan. I called all the caddies I had over the past year—spending long hours on the phone to do so—and got them to sign affidavits testifying to my proper conduct on the course. Not one caddie said he ever saw me do anything illegal on the greens, and those fellows were near me all the time in tournaments.

The LPGA's legal counsel stalled on one matter after another. I remember Carol Mann, who subsequently became LPGA president, openly questioning the tactics and strategy of the LPGA's line of defense. But the endless phone calls and letters to my lawyers continued throughout the summer. I must have averaged two hours a day on the phone.

My lawyers were super. I'll never forget the efforts of John Russell, Gene Partain, Jerry Olshinsky and Larry Kill. The case became a crusade for them. They told me they worked harder on that lawsuit than anything else in their careers.

In an effort to have the lawsuit settled on the anti-trust aspects of that infraction, by the judge himself and without a jury, we requested the court to issue a summary judgment on behalf of the plaintiff (me). An oral argument was made before the court on January 4, 1973, and briefs were filed February 26 and March 2.

Now all we could do was wait.

On June 21, 1973, the second most important legal development of the whole affair occurred. Judge Moye granted the summary judgment on the grounds that the members of the LPGA's executive board, who were all tour players, had engaged in a *per se* unlawful group boycott and restraint of trade. It was a clear violation of Section I of the Sherman Act.

I think these words from the court order are pertinent:

"The suspension [of Jane Blalock] was imposed upon plaintiff by defendants Sullivan, Rankin, Craft, Zavichas and Miller in the exercise of their completely unfettered, subjective discretion as is evident from the fact that they had initially imposed upon plaintiff only probation and a fine, but then, without hearing from plaintiff, determined to impose the suspension at issue here. Furthermore, the suspension was imposed by competitors of plaintiff who stand to gain financially from plaintiff's exclusion from the market."

The judge added, "The arrangement in this case is illegal *per se*. Consequently, it is not necessary that it inquire as to the reasonableness of the suspension."

The LPGA had attempted to bring in the suspension of Jack Molinas by the National Basketball Association many years ago as a precedent. Molinas was suspended by the then NBA commissioner, Maurice Podoloff, on a gambling violation. The judge discarded that notion, explaining, "The suspension was not imposed by Molinas' competitors."

Permission to appeal the summary judgment, as sought by the LPGA, was denied on August 6, 1973. And with that, for all practical purposes, the case was over. We had won. The only issue unresolved was the question of *quantum*. Money. In a case of this type, the losers can be made to pay the winner's legal fees. There was also the matter of my $5 million suit. It would all be settled at a later date, by jury trial.

The summary judgment was announced on the Friday of the Heritage Village Classic at Southbury, Conn. It became the most important issue of that tournament. Susie Berning won by four shots. But she grumbled, "They always follow Janie, no matter what she's doing. She's not playing well, but still she draws the galleries." I tied for third place that week, which I felt was rather good, considering the circumstances.

I think the resentment arising out of the court's decision was definitely a factor in an incident that took place during the U.S. Women's Open the next month at Rochester, N.Y.

On the first hole of that tournament, I had a birdie putt of eight feet, which I left two inches short of the cup. One of my playing partners, an amateur named Janet Coles, and a marshal named J. Richard Wilson both claimed that I had stubbed the second putt and had actually taken three strokes on the green. My other playing partner, Carole Jo Skala, said she had observed nothing illegal.

The dispute was reported to P. J. Boatwright, executive director of the U.S. Golf Association (the Women's Open is run by the USGA, not

the LPGA). Boatwright investigated at the conclusion of the round, declared there were no irregularities and permitted me to sign my card. He added that the incident was considered closed.

Nearly two months later, I was notified that the LPGA's executive board planned to hold a hearing on the incident. This was in clear violation of Rule 11 of the Rules of Golf, which states that a Committee's decision on any dispute is considered final.

Judge Moye ordered that no action could be taken by the LPGA on the issue and threw it out. But it was one more thing I had to live with through the rest of the summer, and the relations between myself and the other girls continued to be strained.

The next step in the legal procession was the trial for damages, which opened August 26, 1974, in Atlanta before Judge Moye and a jury. It was brief and anti-climactic.

The trial began on a Monday morning. It lasted less than two days. Both sides had prepared extensively in the event the trial brought in everything involved in the cheating charges and the lawsuit. We had depositions from all sorts of people testifying to my good character. The other side had testimony to the contrary. It would have made a very interesting trial had the judge sought to cover everything, but instead he restricted it to the anti-trust aspect—the restraint of trade that occurred when the LPGA prevented me from competing at Baltimore.

If the jury had decreed no monetary reward, it would have been a crushing defeat for me. I had legal fees of about $220,000, plus all the expenses I had run up commuting in and out of Atlanta and New York over the two-year period.

One of the most important contributions to my case during the trial was made by Ferdinand K. Levy, dean of the College of Industrial Management at Georgia Tech. He produced an involved manuscript of statistics relating to my previous performance in tournament play and the comparative performances of my tour rivals.

In his extensive and comprehensive report, Mr. Levy concluded that had I been allowed to participate in the Lady Carling Open at Baltimore, I would have won it. The odds against any one player winning a single tournament are substantial, but Mr. Levy had all the statistics to back up his contention.

The jury was, of course, given the complete sequence of events, beginning with the late-night meeting at the Melrose Motel in Louisville, through the meetings at Pine Needles and Baltimore, the temporary restraining order, the permanent injunction, the summary judgment and the constant harassment by the LPGA. I was on the witness stand myself for two hours, going over the same material.

Finally, it was over and the jury went out to make its decision. I tried to eat lunch while they deliberated, but I was so nervous there was no way. About three hours later as we were standing around the lobby waiting, word came that the jury was ready to return. It was just like you'd see on the old Perry Mason Show. I literally held my breath as the foreman stood up and dramatically announced the verdict.

The lonely vigil. I had plenty of moments like this.

First, I was awarded the $4,500 first place money for the Lady Carling Open, which was trebled under anti-trust law to $13,500. Second, the LPGA had to pay all its own legal fees, which came to more than $200,000, plus another $100,000 to my lawyers. I'm proud to say my lawyers accepted a settlement of $98,000 and closed their files, even though their actual bill came to around $220,000.

The final settlement left me with a net deficit of approximately $40,000. I had paid my lawyers about $25,000 in out of pocket expenses during the two years between the suspension and the trial, plus all my own expenses of travel and phone calls relating to the lawsuit. Even if I had been awarded $5 million, we had no way of ever collecting anything like that from the LPGA. The money simply wasn't there. If it had been, the LPGA would have become bankrupt. That would have meant the end of the tour.

The decision has had a far-reaching effect throughout the field of professional sports, focusing on the dangers involved in creating a situation in restraint of trade. It also resulted in a thorough restructuring of the LPGA hierarchy. No longer could a board of players discipline their fellow competitors. We now have a smoothly functioning advisory board of corporate executives who work together with two player representatives. This board reports to our new commissioner, Ray Volpe, who has been a bastion of strength throughout the steady expansion and greatly increased stature of the LPGA.

One of my reasons for writing this book was to emphasize the fact that I did not cheat. I've been saying that in interviews all over the country during the past few years, but I've never had a national audience for that statement. I'll never be fully vindicated because of the nature of the trial. People will always wonder and have their doubts. But it's something I'll have to live with. I have my own peace of mind, and that's most important to me.

I passed up the post-trial celebration in Atlanta and flew immediately to Kansas City to compete in the Southgate Ladies Open at the Leawood South Country Club in Prairie Village, Kan. How that tournament eventually concluded is a story in itself.

Rain prevented me from playing a practice round on the Wednesday before the tournament, but we did get the pro-am in on Thursday. When the tournament started Friday morning, I was concerned about how I would play. I was struggling with a cross-current of emotions. Happy and relieved, naturally, to have won the trial, I was also experiencing a noticeable letdown, which wasn't surprising. The trial had been a long time in coming.

I shot 70 in the first round, one stroke behind Kathy Whitworth. I was happy with that. My game seemed quite solid. On the second round, I was two under par on the front nine and then I made birdies on the 10th, 11th and 12th holes. Coming off the 12th green, I had a five-stroke lead in the tournament.

But then, as we were standing on the 13th tee, a storm suddenly struck the area. It was more like a tornado. Leawood South was better suited to a canoe race, and play was suspended for the day.

Tournament officials decided to count scores that day for the first nine holes of play only, which meant I had lost those three birdies on 10, 11 and 12. Sue Roberts had picked up a late birdie on the front nine, so my lead was now down to one stroke.

The plan was to play the last 27 holes on Sunday, with a shotgun start in the morning. I started on the 11th hole. Sue Roberts had chipped in on 18 for a birdie, so by the time I reached my ninth hole of the day, No. 10, I was one stroke behind Sue. And the weather was turning bad again.

I had a 10-foot putt for a birdie on that 10th hole, and I also had a feeling this was going to be the end of the tournament. It had started to rain hard, so we could play only nine of the 27 scheduled holes that day. I saw no way they could get the last round in the following day, either. We were practically at flood stage.

Standing over the putt, I said to myself, "You'd better make this one." I took a good, square stance, brought the clubhead back slowly and accelerated through the ball. I didn't look up until I heard it plop into the cup.

When the rains washed out any chance to play on Monday, Sue Roberts and I were declared the co-champions of the Ladies Southgate Open, with scores of 142. We each got a check for $4,375 and the tournament counted as an official victory for both of us.

Considering the trial and the tournament, I had set an unofficial LPGA record: two big wins the same week. They were both very sweet.

Did I say my life was full of ironies? In 1976, the Augusta National Golf Club filed a lawsuit seeking an injunction against the use of the name Ladies Masters for one of our LPGA tournaments at Moss Creek Plantation on Hilton Head Island. The Augusta people felt it was an infringement on their Masters tournament.

Among those testifying for Augusta National at the trial, held before U.S. District Court Judge Anthony A. Alaimo in Augusta, were Arnold Palmer and Clifford Roberts, the longtime Masters chairman.

The LPGA was interested in helping the tournament sponsor, Northwestern Mutual Life Insurance Co., to retain the Ladies Masters name. Commissioner Ray Volpe wanted one player to represent the women's tour at the trial. Guess who he picked?

I felt right at home in the courtroom, having had so much experience. I testified that the tournament was a first-class operation, devoid of any commercial aspects, and a quality addition to the tour. I felt the sponsor was entitled to use the name Ladies Masters.

Well, we lost the case. The tournament is now formally known as the Women's International, although the players still call it the Ladies Masters. I was proud to be the tour spokesperson for the LPGA. It was an indication that some of the old wounds have healed, after all.

101

7.

PRESSURE GOLF

We all suffer and sweat in the crunch of competition. Not long ago I was playing a social round in Florida with a lady friend, an amateur with a handicap of about 20. We had a little wager going—$2 for each nine, with strokes. On the 17th green she looked nervously at a six-foot putt, stepped back and groaned. "Oh, this is awful," she said. "My stomach is like a knot. You're so fortunate, Janie. On the tour you must face these problems so often they don't bother you."

Is she kidding?

I've been in situations on the tour where I was scared to death. My stomach had butterflies, my legs were rubbery, my hands felt clammy and my mouth was so dry it felt like the morning after an all-night party. I recall many times when the tension was so great my jawbone was quivering, and I found myself gnashing my teeth audibly.

Professional or amateur, no golfer is ever immune to pressure. How do we overcome it?

I've tried just about everything. Golf is really a cruel game. In football you can release your frustrations by crashing into somebody. In tennis you can put that extra juice on a forehand or rush the net. In golf you don't have those options.

The best ways I know to combat tension are to do deep knee bends on the tee, or shake your hands vigorously before taking the shot. That gets the blood flowing again and loosens the knots. On the greens, sometimes I pace around to inspect the putt from all angles. I don't actually see anything, but it looks like I know what I'm doing and sometimes it takes my mind off the importance of the putt.

Once you're in the furnace however, the best thing to have going for you is a fierce desire to win. In eight years on the tour, I've had more than my share of tight finishes. Sometimes I pulled it out, sometimes I didn't, but I remember each one vividly. You learn from those experiences, especially when you lose.

I'll never forget the Women's Civitan Open at Dallas in 1973. I lost it because the pressure got to me and restricted my swing, costing me a tournament I should have won.

I was defending champion at Dallas that year, having beaten Kathy Whitworth in that acrimonious playoff in 1972. Kathy was playing well in this one, too, leading the tournament. With five holes remaining in the final round, I was only one stroke behind. I was sure I could catch her.

On the 14th hole, I had a 10-foot putt for a birdie that looked so simple my mind was envisioning the ball dropping in before I stroked it.

But the putt lipped out. On the 15th hole, I had a 15-footer for a birdie, hit it perfectly and missed. Time was running out.

Standing on the 16th fairway, about 115 yards from the green, I asked my caddie for the pin placement. "Front center," he replied. I hit a 9-iron shot to the front center. Unfortunately, my caddie was wrong. The pin was placed toward the back of the green, leaving me a putt of 30 feet.

Anxious and upset, I charged the putt and hit it four feet past the pin. Then I missed it coming back. Bogey. I could feel my nerves waxing raw and edgy. It had been a tough year, with the lawsuit still unsettled. The strain was clearly affecting me.

On the 17th hole, I had a downhill approach shot of 140 yards. Normally, I'd hit an 8-iron in that situation. I guess I wasn't thinking very clearly because I took a 7-iron, then made a terrible swing. I did what so many amateurs do under stress: I failed to complete the backswing. I pulled the shot and the ball bounded off a mound to the left of the green. I bogeyed that hole, too, and lost by a stroke.

The moral of that story is that under pressure you must make absolutely sure you complete your backswing. Take the club back slowly, extend the arms fully and hesitate a moment at the top before starting the downswing. In other words, don't hurry the swing.

For the pure agony of sustained tension, I don't suppose I've ever experienced anything like the 1974 Colgate-Dinah Shore tournament at Mission Hills. It was the most exciting day of my career, and the fact it was on national television only heightened the drama—and the pressure.

With nine holes to play on the final round, I was six strokes behind Sandra Haynie, who was with me in the last threesome, and four behind Jo Ann Prentice, in the group ahead. I picked up a stroke with a 30-foot birdie putt on the 10th hole, and chipped in on 12. On the 17th, a par-3, I hit my tee shot one foot from the pin. When first Jo Ann and then Sandra bogeyed that hole, I was only one stroke behind them both going into 18, a par-5 with water surrounding the green.

I tried to think only of taking the club back slowly and staying down through the ball on the drive, and I hit it solidly. After a good 4-wood second shot, I was left with a 9-iron to the green. I made a perfect swing, extending the clubhead straight through at the target, and hit the ball five feet from the flag.

In the ABC television tower behind the green, Dave Marr made a friendly $1 bet with Cathy Duggan, one of our tour players who was doing TV commentary, that I would miss the putt.

"You don't know Janie," Cathy replied, and the bet was on. I didn't take much time lining up that putt. I stroked it crisply, accelerating my left hand through the ball. It fell in for a birdie. Dave Marr signed that dollar bill for Cathy.

Off the three of us went to the 14th hole for the start of a sudden-death playoff. We were still on network television, and you think there

A study in frustration. Sometimes they just won't drop.

wasn't a little sweating as we teed it up? I was so nervous I could hardly get the club back. We all got our pars on 14. On 15, I hit a 4-iron approach shot 15 feet above the hole. Sandra and Jo Ann were both on the fringe. Sandra left her putt six feet short and Jo Ann rolled hers five feet past. Standing over my putt, I told myself, "Don't charge it." It was a dangerous downhill putt. I nudged the ball within two inches of the cup. Sandra missed to fall out of the playoff, but Jo Ann made hers.

On the 16th, a strong par-4 hole, I hit a long drive and put a 6-iron shot on the green, 25 feet away. Jo Ann's tee shot flew into a tree, but the ball caromed back onto the fairway. She smacked a 3-wood to the back fringe of the green. Two more pars, and on to 17.

The 17th is a difficult par-3 requiring a long iron. Jo Ann, who had the honor, hit a super shot, four feet from the flag. Now the pressure was on me. I wanted desperately to hit mine inside of Jo Ann's ball, but it finished 12 feet away. I missed the putt. There was nothing I could do except stand there and watch Jo Ann putt. She knocked it in, and it was all over.

In the confusion that followed, with the gallery scrambling around us, Jo Ann and I never did get around to shaking hands. That was interpreted by some as a sign of animosity between us, a residue of bitter feeling resulting from my lawsuit. It wasn't the case at all. I tried to reach Jo Ann and congratulate her, but I was unable to because of the crush of traffic and the general chaos.

The two of us had a sequel later in the year, at the Lady Errol Classic in Apopka, Fla. I came from behind again, with birdies on 10, 11, 12 and 17, to tie Jo Ann and set up another sudden-death playoff. We both had the feeling we had been there before.

I won that playoff on the first extra hole, with a downhill birdie putt of 15 feet. This time I made sure there would be no repetition of the incident at Palm Springs. I walked over to Jo Ann, took her outstretched hand and shook it heartily so everyone could see.

Sudden-death playoffs are searing on the nervous system. At the completion of regulation play, there is always a lot of confusion and excitement. Everyone's running around shouting. I try to get away by myself for a few moments before the playoff gets underway, but we generally have only about five minutes because it's late in the day and darkness is closing in.

One of the most memorable playoffs I was ever involved in took place in the 1975 Colgate Triple Crown at Mission Hills. It was the climax of a long and hectic struggle merely to qualify for the tournament.

The Triple Crown is the most exclusive event in women's golf. Only nine of the top players are invited to compete, based on their performance in three Colgate-sponsored tournaments: the Dinah Shore, the European Open and the Far East Open. We play it at Mission Hills. It's only 36 holes, and the last round is nationally televised.

To qualify for the 1975 Triple Crown, held in December, I had to play well in the Far East Open in Australia the previous week. I shot 73 the first round and 74 the second, which placed me in a borderline qualifying position going into the final round. The critical hole on the last day was the 12th. I had chipped 15 feet past the flag, and as I waited my turn to putt, I had a little heart-to-heart talk with myself. "You didn't travel 15,000 miles to blow your chance," I said. "You're going to have to make this putt." I tried to remember the fundamentals of a good putting stroke, and I holed it. I made two birdies coming in and finished sixth in the overall compilation of the three tournaments, good enough for a ticket to Mission Hills.

In the first round of the Triple Crown I shot 71, one stroke behind the leader, JoAnne Carner. In the second and final round I was paired with Sandra Palmer and Carol Mann. Carner, Joann Washam and Judy Rankin were in the threesome behind us. I was moving along smoothly until we reached the 14th, a par-3 with water on the right and out-of-bounds on the left. It's one of the most difficult par-3 holes I've seen.

Instead of playing the hole carefully, as I did the first round when I took a bogey, I attacked it. On the tee I looked down at the ball and said, "Little fellow, you're going for a ride." I hit a crisp iron shot and got my par, a real accomplishment for me on that hole.

On the 15th tee I noticed that Carner, Rankin and Washam were all two under par for the tournament. I was one under. On the 17th, another tough par-3, I made my best swing of the year. Remembering to complete the backswing, which is never all that easy under pressure, I hit a perfect 3-iron shot that finished eight feet from the cup. I made the putt, and even though I missed a 10-foot birdie putt on 18 that would have won the tournament right there, I finished in a three-way tie for the lead with Carner and Rankin.

We went into a sudden-death playoff. Talk about pressure! I can think of easier ways to earn a paycheck. JoAnne Carner and Judy Rankin are as tough and competitive as any two athletes anywhere. On the first playoff hole after the customary hectic five-minute wait, I hit a good drive and then a really fine 6-iron shot that wound up 12 feet from the flag. JoAnne and Judy each missed their birdie putts. Now it was up to me.

The line was dead straight. It was late in the day, so the grass was heavy. My only thought was, "Hit it firmly." The ball rolled in, and through the tears in my eyes I looked for my mom and dad in the gallery. It was a wonderful finish to the day, and to the year.

I have described some situations where a competitive temperament has helped me immeasurably, and I already know what you're thinking. How does someone acquire such a characteristic? How do I force myself to meet a challenge successfully?

Well, you've got to remember that I can't make every putt I want. If I did, I'd win every tournament. But there are times, crucial times, when I can concentrate so completely that it seems like I'm willing the ball into the hole. I've always been a good last-round player, and I'm proud of my record of winning the tournaments I have been in a position to win.

My background suggests that I had a competitive nature long before I began playing golf. This has been an asset, but I've gone beyond that to develop a sense of willpower that has created a reservoir of confidence in the crucible of a close finish.

An example was the Colgate Triple Crown held in January, 1977. I was the defending champion, based on my victory in December, 1975, and I was determined to win it again. Not only for the prestige, the cash and the new Plymouth Volare station wagon, but also to launch my 1977 tour on a high note.

For three days before the tournament, I built myself into a state of emotional readiness. I was psyching myself up, mentally preparing for the competition. Not everyone can do that. I'm fortunate that I can. I'm not very good company during this time. I like to stay secluded, with no distractions or frivolities.

The end result is that I virtually *will* myself into a trance. I call it a mellow feeling. No highs, no lows. It's like I'm in a world of my own. I walk slowly, and try to keep my emotions on an even keel. I get angry on the course over a bad shot, sure, but I'm not about to display it by slamming my club to the ground or kicking a tee marker.

Despite that protective shroud, my emotions can still be boiling inside. I played consistent golf in the 1977 Triple Crown, but on the 16th hole of the final round I made a terrible first putt that left me with a five-footer for my par. I was scared. My caddie, Paul English, started to advise me on the putt but I cut him off with the remark, "No, let me handle it." That putt was the most crucial stroke I had, and I made it. I didn't need to make a birdie on 18 to win, but I felt mellow enough that if I had to, I could.

Speaking of pressure situations, I'd like to bring up a point I've often heard discussed among good athletes. It's a little-known fact that the most critical time in a competition, the real moment of truth, may often occur early in the day. Nobody else might recognize it, but the turning point is there. If you pull it off, the other pieces fall into place. If you don't, you know it's going to be an uphill battle.

Joan Joyce, the softball pitcher, says that for her the critical point comes in the first inning of the game. She wants desperately to shut the other team out in the first inning, with three strikeouts, if possible. It gives her an edge. Billie Jean King says her crucial time in tennis is the seventh game of a set. My own pivotal hole varies. It may be the second, or the 12th, as it was during the Triple Crown qualifying in Australia. But I can always recognize when the time has come, when I must bear down harder.

I've often wondered if the Oakland Raiders felt that way in the first period of the 1977 Super Bowl, when they recovered a Minnesota fumble on their own two-yard line. The Raiders took command of the game at that point, and the Vikings looked like a beaten team.

I'm a football fan, and as I sat there in the Rose Bowl and watched while Oakland built a substantial lead, I thought back to my own experience in the Dallas tournament in 1976. It's always a strain to lead during the final round, and the pressure can be compounded when you lead it all the way. Occasionally, however, your tempo is so good that you just blow everyone else right out of the ball park. That happened to me at Dallas, where I won the tournament by nine strokes.

There is no middle ground for me in my feeling for a course. I either love it or I hate it. My record shows that I play certain courses very well, others very poorly. I've won three times at Mission Hills and twice each at Indian Hills, Errol Estate and Brookhaven. Brookhaven, the site of the Dallas tournament, is definitely one of my favorite

My first Triple Crown, one of the happiest days of my career.

courses. It is well designed and appealing, requires a strong mid-iron game and the greens are true.

The background of my 1976 Dallas victory is hardly a model of proper tournament preparation. I wouldn't suggest it as a regular diet, but in this case it must have been just right for me.

The tournament preceding Dallas was the Jerry Lewis Muscular Dystrophy Classic at the Rail Golf Club in Springfield, Ill. It wound up in a four-way playoff that went three holes before Sandra Palmer finally won. I finished fifth, three strokes behind the leaders. I wanted to spend a few days in New England before going down to Dallas, and since there was no commercial flight out of Springfield on Sunday night, Carol Mann and I chartered a plane to Chicago. It cost us $125 apiece, but it was worth it. I flew into Hartford that night and then drove on to Meriden (Conn.) to be with our softball team for a few days.

It was a relaxing time, watching the girls practice and play softball, and I didn't leave until Wednesday morning on the five-hour flight from Hartford to Dallas. I got there just in time to play in the pro-am. Brookhaven has 36 holes, and the pro-am was played at the course we did not use for the tournament. It rained all Thursday morning. I got out late that afternoon and played nine holes. I didn't putt the greens, because they had been softened by the rain and I knew they'd be firmer the next day. So I teed it up on Friday with a minimum of preparation.

Although I was physically tired from all the traveling, my mental attitude was good. The pressure is always stronger until you win your first tournament of the year, and I had won at Wheeling, W. Va., a few weeks earlier, so I was loose and confident. My only thought on the first tee in the opening round was this: "Today, I'm not going to start out with any 76 and spot the field nine shots. I've had enough of those shaky first rounds. Today, the field is going to spot me nine shots." I birdied the first hole, picked up four birdies on the back nine and shot 67. I didn't have a nine-stroke lead, but I had four, over Sandra Post, and that's not a bad start.

The next day I birdied the first hole again. I was hitting everything into the hole. I made four birdie putts of more than 10 feet, and par putts of four, six, eight and 10 feet. Now I was pulling away from the field. I shot another 67 and had my nine-stroke lead. It was the first time I had ever played two straight competitive rounds without a bogey.

Coming down the back nine on that second round, I kept thinking, "Just keep whittling away. Be tough. When you've got somebody down, stomp on them. The greater cushion you can build today, the easier things will be tomorrow."

It was like Raymond Floyd at the 1976 Masters. The only way he could have lost on the final day was to collapse completely, and then someone else still would have needed an exceptional round to catch him. I was nervous that Saturday night, though. Kathy Whitworth was 10 strokes behind me; I knew she'd be making a real run the next day.

So the pressure was there, even with a nine-shot lead. I was very shaky early in the final round. I scuffed a wedge shot over the first green and had to make a six-foot putt to save par. On the fifth green I three-putted from 25 feet, my first bogey in 40 holes. I took bogeys on the ninth and 10th, both tough holes into the wind, but I still led by seven with eight holes to play. Something like Palmer at Olympic in the '66 Open? I didn't want to think about that.

Well, it was one of those days. I shot birdies on 11, 12, 13 and 14 and that was it. Kathy Whitworth's 70 was the low round of the day, which gave her second place at 214, but I shot 71 for a 205 and the nine-stroke win. It was by far my best performance of the year. Later I checked my biorhythmic chart for that week, and everything was a strong plus. No wonder I felt so great.

People asked me after that tournament if there was anything that a golfer trailing by nine shots can do to break the leader's momentum. Can a little gamesmanship come into play? Sometimes it can, but not that day. The only thing anyone could have done was try to birdie every hole and hope I would have nothing but trouble. There's not much they could have said.

I do remember one time at St. Paul in 1973, when Sandra Palmer said something to me that influenced the final outcome. It was a much closer finish than Dallas. Sandra had a two-shot lead going into the final round, but after shooting 32 on the front nine I led by two. On the 10th tee Sandra turned to me and said, "You're sure making a lot of good putts." It might have been an intentional effort to disrupt my concentration. I got to the 10th green and began thinking, "Gee, I have been making some good putts." I hadn't been concerned about how I made them, I just had a good putting rhythm. Suddenly that rhythm was gone. Sandra won the tournament.

If that ever happens to me again, I'll just smile and say, "I'm going to keep on making them"—and hope that I do.

That kind of tactic is probably more widespread in match play, a game most of the tour women hate. We don't play much of it and that's just as well. Match play is a personal thing. You're trying to eliminate your opponent, send her on down the road. Feelings can easily become strained.

In match play, every hole is like a sudden-death playoff. I've seen experienced pros get so tense they become almost hyper-ventilated. When that happens, you must pull yourself aside, take some deep breaths and drink some water to wash down that cotton-dry feeling.

My first experience at match play on the tour was such a calamity it left me scarred for months. It was the 1972 Sears Women's Classic at Port St. Lucie, Fla., our only match play event of that year. I was leading Betsy Cullen 2-up with three holes to play. I shot them in two pars and a birdie. The only problem was that Betsy finished birdie-birdie-eagle. She beat me with a long putt on 18. I was so crushed I swore I'd never again enter a match play tournament, but eventually the pain wore off.

Much more satisfying was the 1976 International Team Mixed

Championship, sponsored by Trans-World International and played in Ireland. Teams composed of men and women professionals represented the United States, England, South Africa and Australia. Raymond Floyd and I were the U.S. entry. It wasn't match play in the strictest sense of the term, but rather what they call stroke match. For example, team A plays team B, the loser dropping out and the winner advancing. The result is not determined hole by hole, but by the number of strokes. It combines features of both games.

Our first match was against Graham Marsh and Jan Stephenson, the Australian team. They are both great players. Raymond and I were four strokes down after the first seven holes at Waterville, but we caught up and eventually won that match by a stroke. In the finals we moved to Killarney and met the South African tigers, Gary Player and Sally Little. We won by eight strokes.

Having some Irish blood in me, it was a wonderful experience playing over there. The people were warm and gracious, and the courses excellent. It was an ideal week's break in the middle of the summer.

Even though we played those matches in total strokes instead of hole by hole, it had a close resemblance to the dominant type of competition for club members. Match play is more practical than stroke play in club tournaments, because one bad hole doesn't have to cost the whole round.

There's always tension, though, and it seems to increase when handicap strokes are involved. The woman who receives the stroke feels she must come through because of the advantage. You've heard the old line, "Partner, you've got a stroke on this one, so make it count." Brrr. I can just see the muscles stiffening. One bad shot breeds another. Instead of coming directly out of trouble and settling for a bogey—a net par which will probably win the hole—the stroke recipient gambles on a heroic shot through the trees and winds up with an eight.

If you start feeling tense, try to slow down your tempo. Walk slower, and take a more leisurely backswing. Avoid the mistake of standing over the ball at address too long. That just promotes more strain. We have a saying on tour, "Let 'er fly." It's something to remember when you're trying to steer the ball around the course in an attempt to keep it in play. Relax, and enjoy the game.

No matter how hard you try to overcome battle nerves, the very structure of tournament golf creates an atmosphere of stress within us all. One day I was playing a social round in Boca Raton with Mrs. Joe Wolfel, whose husband is an engineer for Pro-Dyne, a golf equipment company. She got to talking about how nervous she becomes in club tournaments.

"My hands get so clammy," she said, "I actually hate to shake hands with my opponent after a round. It's embarrassing." I told her that we have the same problem on the tour, on every hole of every round of the year.

Concentration, so vital to good golf, is another problem in club competition. It's tough to concentrate while you're inquiring about your partner's children, or what you're going to have for dinner that night. There are times when you just have to ignore those distractions.

I was talking about this on the course one day with Carl Yastrzemski of the Boston Red Sox. (Carl threw a 79 at me with a 14 handicap). I asked him how he could concentrate at bat while some of those Fenway Park fans were booing him.

"By blocking them out of my mind," he replied. "I don't even hear them. When I'm going good they cheer and when I'm in a slump they boo. I just don't pay any attention. It's me and the pitcher out there, and the only thing I'm concentrating on is the ball coming in."

Yastrzemski is one of the most competitive persons I've ever known. In the clutch, he's at his best.

In summing up this chapter on the pressures of competition, I'd like to share with you a poem that I refer to often when the going gets tough. I clipped it out of a magazine and keep it in my golf bag.

"If you think you are beaten,
You are.
If you think you dare not,
You don't.
If you'd like to win,
But think you can't,
It's almost a cinch you won't.
If you think you'll lose,
You're lost.
For in this world we find
Success begins with a fellow's will;
It's all in the state of mind.
Life's battles don't always go
To the stronger or fleeter man;
But sooner or later the man who wins
Is the one who thinks he can."

8.

ON THE GREEN: WOMEN VS. MEN

For years it was considered fashionable among the general public to regard the women pros as better putters than the men. We certainly couldn't hit the ball as far, but we were shooting good scores. The mystique of our putting superiority was flattering, and we cultivated it. Nobody who ever saw Kathy Whitworth at the peak of her game would challenge it, either. Kathy could match almost anyone alive at the art of getting the ball up and down.

Then we started appearing more frequently on television, playing tough courses. We were putting on greens that were not only huge, but slick and undulating. The television viewers saw us taking three from the edge and missing six-foot birdie putts. They began wondering if we were such great putters after all.

That sudden skepticism was fanned by two members of the national media, neither of whom has ever had much time for women's golf. Bob Rosburg, former PGA champion who became a TV golf analyst, declared that women were actually lousy putters because we lacked emotional stability. Dan Jenkins quoted Rosburg in a *Sports Illustrated* article right after the 1976 Colgate-Dinah Shore tournament, and soon we were hearing from everyone how badly we putted. Well, let's set a few things straight on that point and then go into the fundamentals that can make better putters of us all.

I'm going to come out right here and say that women are not equal to men as putters—we are better. I watch the men on TV as often as possible, and I see them missing more crucial putts than we do. They're missing them, moreover, on immaculate greens, where a properly stroked putt should roll true. You ought to see some of the greens we play on the LPGA tour! It's a miracle we hole as many putts as we do.

A few years ago, at Springfield, Ohio, the greens were so bad we were entitled to pick up after the first putt. Everybody who missed the first one got an automatic two putts. We held our LPGA Championship in 1976 on terrible greens at Pine Ridge Golf Club in Baltimore, a public course which saw heavy play. The greens were grainy at Dallas, bumpy at Cleveland and shaggy at St. Paul. Although the conditions are improving each year, we seldom play the same type of greens on successive weeks.

In the 1976 National Golf Day Round of the Champions, Sandra

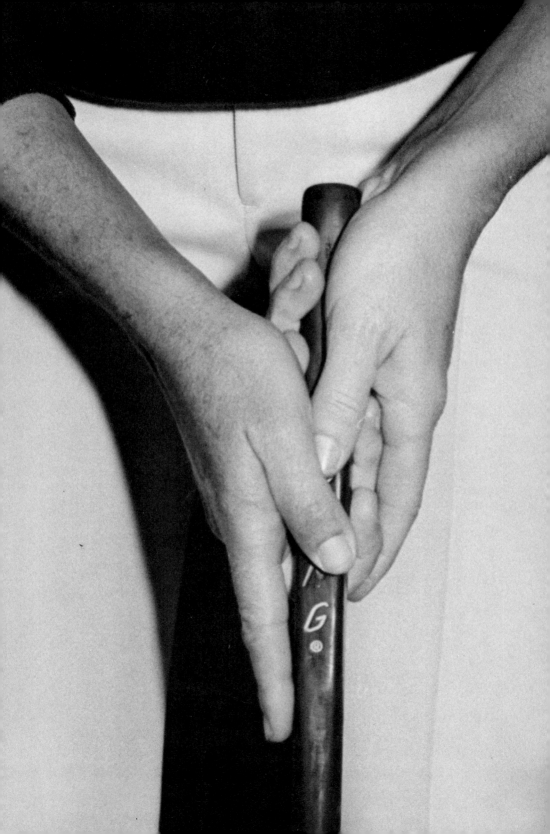

Palmer and Kathy Whitworth represented the LPGA against Jack Nicklaus and Lou Graham. The event was held at Congressional Country Club in Washington, D.C., site of the PGA Championship a few months later. Sandra told me later that during the round Nicklaus and Graham complained frequently that the greens were slow and difficult to read.

"I was thinking the whole time how fast they were, and how much better than the greens we normally play on," Sandra said. While neither of the two women putted especially well that day, they felt the conditions were very favorable. They considered the greens at Congressional comparable to the best we see throughout the year.

Since putting is about 40 percent of golf, we spend a lot of time practicing. We know that a good putting round can atone for errors on the tee and on the fairway. I recommend that you practice, too, while keeping in mind the basics of a sound putting stroke.

First, let's consider the stance. I try to keep it as simple and square as possible. In other words, the shoulders, hips and feet should be in the same line, and the blade of the putter perfectly square to that line. This eliminates the need to compensate, which can only lead to trouble.

The eyes should be directly over the ball. You can test this by dropping a ball from right in front of your eyes. It should fall directly upon the ball you are lining up to putt. Putting is controlled by eye-hand coordination, and the muscles respond to the eye line of the putt. If the eyes are not directly over the ball, you start compensating by aiming right and pulling the ball left.

The grip is a personal thing. Use whatever feels comfortable, although the palm of the right hand and the back of the left should be facing the target. I favor a reverse overlap, with both thumbs on top and the pressure supplied by the last three fingers of the left hand. I overlap the little finger of my right hand between the middle and ring fingers of the left hand, with the forefinger of the left hand riding down the shaft for greater control. When I first came out on the tour, I missed a lot of short putts, pulling some and pushing others. I found that dropping the finger down the shaft provides just a little extra firmness as the putter moves through the ball.

How tightly should you grip the putter? Firmly enough so the hands don't move on the handle, but lightly enough to eliminate any tension. A light grip promotes greater sensitivity and feel for distance. Bob Toski likes to compare the grip on the putter to that of a surgeon's hold on his scalpel.

The critical key is *tempo*. You have to keep it consistent, regardless of the condition of the green. Take the club back slowly, but strike the ball firmly enough to accelerate the putter blade through the ball to the hole. I think of the putting stroke as a "tick-tock" tempo, with the

The Blalock reverse overlap grip, with my thumbs riding on top of the shaft. This isn't for everyone because the grip is an individual matter. Use whatever is comfortable for you.

Here's the putting rhythm I recommend: tick-*tock*, tick-*tock*, with the emphasis on the left hand leading through the stroke.

emphasis on the "tock." Tick-*tock*, tick-*tock*. That overcomes any tendency to quit on the stroke, which is fatal.

Johnny Revolta has improved my putting considerably. One of his favorite pieces of advice is: "Don't manipulate the putter." He insists that his pupils work at keeping the loft constant throughout the stroke. Opening the face tends to raise the loft, and closing it reduces the loft. You'll never get the ball rolling smoothly unless you keep the blade square to the path. Your hands, of course, must work together.

Fast greens terrorize many higher-handicap players, who find they often have difficulty controlling the ball. One reason is that they take too long a backswing and then quit on the stroke. When the greens are slick I make sure I take a shorter backswing and then accelerate through the ball.

On grainy, Poa annua-infested greens we encounter often on the tour, you have to firm up the grip and take a slightly longer stroke. You want more topspin to keep the ball moving over the bad spots, so strike higher on the ball to get it rolling. On good greens, simply keep the blade low at all times—low on the backswing and low as it accelerates through the ball.

On downhill putts, you'll want to deaden the impact, so the ball doesn't roll 10 feet past the hole. I learned to do that by striking the ball with either the toe or heel of the putter. On a downhill putt with a severe right-to-left break, I make contact with the heel; with a severe left-to-right break, I make contact with the toe. This enables the ball to fight the terrain and roll with the natural break of the green.

This was the technique that won the 1974 Lady Errol Classic in Florida. As I mentioned earlier, Jo Ann Prentice and I had tied for the lead at the end of regulation play and went into sudden death on the first hole. The nines were flopped around for that tournament, so we teed off on what is normally the 10th hole, a par-4. I hit my approach shot 15 feet above the pin, which left me with a slippery downhill putt and a 12-inch left-to-right break. I was looking at a very possible three-putt green. Taking a short backswing, only two inches, I struck the ball with the toe of the putter and rolled it into the cup for a birdie that ended the playoff right there.

Golf is a capricious game, however, and in another incident my application of the toe-stroke nearly backfired on me. It occurred on the 16th green at Mission Hills during the final round of the Colgate Triple Crown in January, 1977. Leading the tournament by one stroke, I had a 25-foot putt from the left fringe that was obviously going to break right. It was downhill, so I struck the ball with the toe of the putter. The ball was hit so gently it lost speed and veered sharply to the right. I had a five-footer for my second putt, but I pulled myself together and knocked it firmly into the hole, as I described in Chapter 7. I parred the last two holes and won the tournament.

The next time you attend an LPGA tournament, stroll over to the practice green and watch the women putt. One thing you seldom see is a wristy stroke. The good putters on the tour are arm putters who keep hand action to a minimum. Arm-putting promotes the consistency we are all constantly seeking.

Is there anything more aggravating than missing a short putt? The stroke is lost forever, and the effect on the mind is one of anger, frustration and uncertainty. The problem is, of course, that we're all expected to make those short putts and the pressure builds. The tendency is to think of the consequences of missing. I try not to do it, but the thought is still there—what if I miss this one? You have to blot that out of your mind. The worst you can do is miss it. Remember, the more positive you think, the more putts you'll sink.

Two pitfalls on the short putt are "wishing" the ball into the hole and "looking" the ball into the hole. "Wishing" is striking the ball so timidly it has no chance. "Looking" is peeking at the hole before the stroke is completed. You have to keep your head still over the ball on any putt, but I try to keep it still for an even longer period of time on all short putts. On putts inside of 10 feet, I never see the ball fall in. I try to stay down on the ball for that fraction of a second longer, until I hear it plop into the cup. And don't let your eyes follow the clubhead on the backstroke. Keep them riveted on the ball.

I don't suppose there is any way to totally eliminate tension in putting, but I certainly try to minimize it by removing the importance of that putt from my mind. When you're playing for the kind of money we do on the tour these days, that's not an easy thing to do. But you must find some way to free the mind from tension and rely on the basic fundamentals of the stroke. And for heaven's sake, remember that club golf is still a game, and the consequences of one missed putt are really not that critical.

We've all seen golfers stand over a putt as if transfixed. That's the best way I know to insure missing it. Once you've read the green to determine the break, and your eyes have told your muscles how hard to hit it, stroke the ball without further indecision. I can cite you three examples, one of which I was involved in. The other two took place during the British Open.

In 1970, on the last hole of the fourth round of the British Open at St. Andrews, Doug Sanders appeared to have the tournament in his pocket. All he needed to do was to get down in two putts. You could almost see Doug licking his chops and counting the financial windfall from what would have been the first major championship of his career.

Sanders left his first putt about 3½ feet short. He seemed uncertain of the break on the second one. He stood over it for a long time, then reached down and flicked away a particle of grass. Now he had to set up over the ball again, and he missed. Jack Nicklaus beat him in the 18-hole playoff the next day, a turning point in the careers of both. Nicklaus, who had not won a major championship since the 1967 U.S. Open at Baltusrol, went on in the next three years to break Bobby Jones' record of 13 majors. Sanders went into decline.

In the 1971 British Open at Royal Birkdale, Lee Trevino was fighting off a late challenge by the dynamic little Oriental, Mr. Lu. It all boiled down to whether Lee could make his second putt on the 72nd hole, a nasty three-footer. Before the television cameras could even focus on him, Lee walked up and stroked that ball firmly into the cup. He wasn't about to agonize over it, as Sanders had done a year earlier.

My experience occurred during the 1974 Colgate-Dinah Shore tournament at Mission Hills. I needed birdies on the last two holes to tie

Jo Ann Prentice and Sandra Haynie for the championship, a pressure-ridden experience I described in the last chapter. I got my birdie on 17, a par-3 hole I usually play well, and hit my approach shot within five feet on 18. As I crossed the bridge leading to the island green, I thought the longer I looked at that putt the longer it would get. I took a quick read, realized it was a straight putt and promptly stroked it in. Jo Ann won the playoff on the fourth extra hole, but I had battled her all the way.

There are days when you strike the ball beautifully, but cannot get the ball into the hole. You just don't seem to have a good stroke. Those are the times when you reach out and try something different, some desperate way to make the putts fall. It happened to me in the 1975 Triple Crown, a tournament where I hit 35 of the 36 greens in regulation figures, but made only three birdies.

On the 17th hole of the second and final round, I hit a 3-iron tee shot eight feet from the hole. By this time, however, I had lost all confidence in my putting stroke. But here I got a lucky break. There was a five-minute delay in play because of a ruling on Carol Mann's tee shot. Instead of spending that time brooding over my shaky putting, I used it to compose my thoughts and pull myself together. "There's got to be some way," I told myself, "that you can make this putt."

Suddenly, in my mind, I pictured Jack Nicklaus hunkering over the ball in that familiar stance. To those who watch him, it appears that Jack is setting up behind the ball, to give himself a better line. Of course! I tried it, and it worked. I made the putt, and won the Triple Crown. Thanks, Jack.

That victory, coming shortly before Christmas, made my entire 1975 season. I won the 1977 Triple Crown later, on the same course, with the most consistent putting I have ever done in any tournament competition. I did not have a single three-putt green in 36 holes, and made 12 putts between four and five feet. Isn't golf a strange game?

Through some good instruction, many hours of practice and occasional improvisations, I have become a reasonably good putter. Sure, I have days when my eye-hand coordination is fuzzy, but I try to let my eyes do the thinking and let my arms swing in relation to what my eyes see.

I would like to add one final piece of advice for the average player. It has become habitual on both the men's and women's tours to mark the ball after the first putt. This is more a psychological gimmick than anything else. I strongly urge the club golfer to walk up and finish the putt, eliminating the needless delay and tension. It will not only speed up play, it will make you a better putter.

9.

THE TROUBLE WITH WOMEN'S GOLF

I don't suppose there is anyone in the country who conducts a more informative and entertaining golf clinic than Patty Berg or Bob Toski. Patty puts on many of her clinics on the day preceding the opening round of our LPGA tour events. Bob has become internationally prominent through the Golf Digest Instruction Schools.

Each has a little comedy act that gets a lot of laughs, although Bob's is done primarily to illustrate the points he and his fellow instructors have been stressing to their pupils. He and Patty are both masters at mimicking the swing of a high-handicapped woman golfer, with all of the stereotyped flaws. Both are hysterically funny.

The sad truth is that women golfers have been ridiculed and maligned for a long time. They not only account for a good share of the revenue in most country clubs, women are largely responsible for the continued growth of golf. The National Golf Foundation says the increase of new golfers among women is 8 percent a year, against a 1 percent increase for the men.

Although I personally feel that women make a tremendous contribution to every facet of golf, we have not been getting a fair shake in weekend starting times, the type of equipment available or in the design of the courses we play.

Let's consider the courses first, because that's the subject that bugs me the most.

Nearly every course in this country was designed for men. From the regular men's tees, those courses are simply too long for women. For years we played from the men's tees, on the tour and in club competition, until someone got the bright idea to build separate tees for the women.

The problem is that in most cases those women's tees are a joke. Instead of being elevated, with special tee grass, they are merely little boxes of short-mown fairway grass, usually stuck on a ridge where you must stand on your ear to address the ball.

Most club women can't reach the green even from those shortened tees. A par-4 hole requires two woods and a short iron. Longer par-5s take three woods and a short iron.

I was interested in a remark by Alice Dye, wife of golf architect Pete Dye and a former Curtis Cup player. She was once asked to name a par-4 that a 15-handicap woman player could reach in a drive and an

8-iron. Alice couldn't think of any. "Women are forced to play most courses," she said, "the way men play Medinah when it's set up for the U.S. Open."

Shorter tees do allow the women some compensation for their drives, but what about the second shot? Suppose that a husband and wife are playing a round together. The wife, driving from the women's tees, hits her shot to about the same place that her husband reaches from the men's tees. The husband may have a 5-iron approach to the green, but the wife must hit a wood to have any chance. That's not my idea of equality.

The USGA has determined that the drive of a scratch-handicap woman carries roughly 30 yards short of a scratch male's drive. To have any opportunity to reach the green, that scratch-handicap woman needs an advantage of at least 60 yards from the shorter tees.

The problem is compounded for the average woman player. There's just no way she can compete with an average male golfer, not the way those piddling concessions called women's tees are constructed on most courses.

The obvious solution is a whole new philosophy of course design. Women's tees should be constructed the same way men's tees are, and they should be placed so that the average woman has a fair chance of reaching the green in three shots on a par-5, in two on a par-4 and in one iron shot on a par-3.

Here's an example of what I mean. Say we have a par-3 hole carrying over water, with the blue championship tees measuring 180 yards and the regular men's tees measuring 170. The women's tee ground should be built at a spot 130 yards from the green, giving her a chance to hit the good iron shot over the water. She can't do that consistently from 150 yards, and it becomes very difficult from 160.

I'm reminded how tough things are for the average woman player every time I return home and play the Portsmouth Country Club. I wear out my woods and long irons. What chance does a 20- or 25-handicap woman member have?

Many new resort courses are being created with proper women's tees. It's fun to play golf under these conditions. If the resorts can do it, why can't municipal courses and country clubs?

When a club tells the superintendent to cut a square of grass and plop down tee markers somewhere out there in the fairway, it cheats the woman golfer. We don't have the opportunity to play the course the way the architect intended it to be played. We are robbed not only of the aesthetic beauty of the course, but of employing any kind of strategy to set up the proper approach. I often see courses where a properly placed woman's tee could afford the dual thrill of beauty and challenge. Instead, we are given the option of playing a muscle game from the men's tees or laying up short of the water with an iron from those raggedy women's tees. What fun is that?

I'm surprised that the women members have put up with this need-

An ideal par-4 hole for women: the 13th, 348 yards, at The Hamlet in Delray Beach, Fla.

less discrimination for as long as they have.

Someday I'd like to design a championship course for women. It would play about 6,000 yards. We could carry the water with a properly played shot, and we wouldn't use our woods and long irons all the time on the fairway. Before my plans ever reach the drawing board, I'll think them out and visualize the holes in my mind. I'll have three sets of tees—long, medium and short. In other words, a course for women of all skills.

The Hamlet in Delray Beach, Fla., is an excellent course for women. Because I live nearby, I play The Hamlet often and enjoy it very much. There are some par-4 holes I can reach with a drive and a short iron, which is a relaxing way to play golf.

My choice of the course that most ideally utilizes women's tees is Boca Rio, in Boca Raton. Ironically, it was built for men, wealthy men who had grown tired of waiting for starting times at their clubs around

Fort Lauderdale. So they built Boca Rio, an elegant course with four sets of tees. I've played Boca Rio several times with Maury Rosen, a member and close friend. We prefer to use the white tees from where the course plays to about 6,500 yards. The views and sight lines are beautiful. Occasionally, we take a golf car and motor along each hole from the championship tees, the view from back there being equally appealing. Boca Rio was built with both aesthetic and shot values incorporated into each set of tees. You rarely see that on a course these days.

One of the reasons I enjoy playing golf with a male amateur whose handicap is 10 is that we both hit the ball about the same distance. In normal weather conditions, my drives carry between 225 and 230 yards. I hit the fairway woods about 200 yards, the 5-iron about 150 yards and the 7-iron about 130. Nothing awesome about that. But I putt reasonably well, and I don't waste many strokes around the greens.

Most of the courses we play on the tour are fairly long. We use the regular men's tees, which means the courses measure around 6,500 yards. I understand they played even longer back in the early days of the LPGA, when Patty Berg and Babe Zaharias were slugging the ball 250 yards with their drivers and then hitting woods to the greens. It couldn't have been much fun for the shorter-hitting women pros.

Mission Hills in Palm Springs is long enough, but the air is thinner in the desert and the ball travels farther. They built new tees for us after the first Dinah Shore tournament, too. For all its challenge, Mission Hills is eminently playable for women.

That's generally more than one can say for the annual site of the U.S. Women's Open. By the time the USGA has that course set up, the holes are long and narrow. The rough along the fairway and around the greens is thick, and the bunkering is severe. The USGA used to allow any amateur with a low handicap to compete without even qualifying, and the rounds usually took six hours and more to complete. Playing in the Women's Open is never much fun.

For several years the USGA put us on second-rate courses in areas that couldn't possibly draw decent galleries. From 1969 through 1971 the Women's Open was held at Pensacola, Fla., Muskogee, Okla., and Erie, Pa. It was 110 degrees one day at Pensacola.

Winged Foot, where we played in 1972, is a great course for men. But it was torturous the way it was set up for women. Susie Berning was the only golfer in the field to break 300.

After drawing good galleries for the Women's Open in 1973 at Rochester, N.Y., we considered boycotting the 1974 tournament at LaGrange, Ill., unless the $40,000 purse was increased. We balked and hassled, and finally agreed to play for $50,000.

In 1975, the Women's Open was assigned to the Atlantic City Country Club with a total purse of $55,000. (Lou Graham made $40,000 himself for winning the Men's Open the same year at Medinah). We protested the token increase, but the USGA claimed we weren't drawing enough people to merit larger purses. Who could draw galleries in Pensacola or Muskogee during July?

On the night I checked into my motel room in Atlantic City, I was watching a television news program that proclaimed Atlantic City as a depressed area, eligible for federal relief funds. That's where we were supposed to draw big galleries?

In 1976, we played for $60,000 at the Rolling Green Golf Club near Springfield, Pa., where the rough was so thick a gorilla couldn't get the ball out. We had our usual one day of television coverage that was so poorly produced it would have been better not to have had it at all.

While the USGA persists in putting the women on the rack in their Open Championship, the LPGA leans to a philosophy that lower scores generate greater response from the general public and more interest from the media. Accordingly, in January 1975 it proclaimed that our tour events would be played from the front tees.

The concept was fine, but I didn't think we had to make a public announcement about it. Let the scores speak for themselves. It didn't make much difference, because the plan lasted about a month. The long hitters griped so loudly that we returned to the old distances.

For the big hitters, a long course offers an incalculable advantage. It leaves 90 percent of the field struggling merely to reach the greens. Any time we're playing a reasonably long course, JoAnne Carner should be whipped if she doesn't win. She consistently drives the ball 260 yards, frequently 270. JoAnne is playing a 7-iron to the green when the rest of us are hitting 3-irons.

Let's shift the focus here from tour golf to the problems encountered in competition by women at their clubs. I've always had a deep interest in women's amateur golf. During my teenage and college years I played a good deal of club golf in New Hampshire.

Watching those women on the course, I developed a good insight into their games. Most of them were too mechanical. They overreacted to instruction. For example, in their group lessons the pro would tell them to bend at the knees. They were so obedient they were practically kneeling. Keep your left arm straight, they were reminded, and they did . . . so stiff it looked frozen.

Playing in pro-ams all over the country, I see so many women trying to force their shots. They try to lift the ball with the swing instead of with the clubface. They are too anxious to strike a good shot, and in their anxiety they hurry the sequence of the swing. I remember Bob Toski telling me, "Don't force the shot. Just let it happen." In other words, let the clubface get the ball into the air.

Another common error is attempting to use the fairway wood in the rough or in a bunker. They are tough shots to pull off. There are times, I do believe, when we expect too much of ourselves. The main thing to concentrate on in the bunker is getting the ball out. That's all, really. Just get the ball out and back into play.

I didn't know much about alignment and setup during my golfing days with the women in New Hampshire, but I learned about it later. And when I did some teaching with Toski and other instructors, I noticed how many women seemed to have a faulty alignment. Ninety percent of them aim to the right of the target.

The best way to overcome that fault is to line up a club on the ground, parallel to the way the pupil is aiming. Then ask the pupil to step back and take a look. It's unbelievable how far off her alignment can be. Golf is tough enough without starting the ball off in the wrong direction. By working to perfect a proper alignment, toward the target, you'll at least give yourself an opportunity to hit the ball straight.

Since this is not intended to be an instructional book, I won't go into the technicalities of the swing. You can get that from your professional. But there is one drill I can't resist including here—a drill to promote good tempo in the swing. *Swing the club with your feet together.* Do it several times before you start your round. Bob Toski, Jim Flick and Peter Kostis use this technique with great success at the Golf Digest Instruction Schools. You can't over-swing in this position, and you'd be surprised how far you can hit the ball with your feet together. It's a marvelous way to develop tempo, as well as balance.

A smooth swing tempo demands another ingredient—the right equipment. I see so many women amateurs attempting to play with men's clubs. No way. Women just aren't strong enough to handle them. The golf industry reports a sharp trend toward lighter clubs at all levels of the game, and this should be a particular help to the woman club player.

It's a sad fact that women have faced a real discrimination problem in golf equipment for a long time. The clubs available to them were never of the same high quality as the men's. While the big companies were putting their best talents and efforts into the manufacture and marketing of top clubs for men, they were turning out women's clubs with prissy names like Lady So-and-So.

Late in 1976 I began using a graphite-shafted driver and I can recommend it highly for women. It's lighter than a steel shaft, and results in more clubhead speed that in turn generates greater distance. I've added at least 15 yards to my drives with the graphite club. But remember this—with the graphite shaft you'll need a club with a heavier swing weight. I prefer a D4 swing-weighted graphite driver, with a regular shaft.

New concepts are constantly evolving in golf instruction, and I think the most significant advances in recent years have been in the area of the game's mental aspect. The best teachers are urging their pupils to develop a candid appraisal of their own games, to attempt the shots they are capable of executing. They call it learning to play within yourself.

Here's an example. If you're a 25-handicapper, you cannot expect to hit a 2-iron shot 180 yards over a bunker to a tightly tucked pin position, with any degree of consistency, if at all. Let the pros take those

Proper alignment seems to be a particular problem for women. To overcome it, line up a club parallel to your intended line of flight.

gambles. Why not lay up with a 5-iron short of the bunker, and then pitch the next shot on the green? You may get down in one putt.

Failure to execute a difficult shot leads to anxiety, and the anxiety results in tension. Soon your game is in tatters. The tension of normal golf competition can be overcome by the confidence you have in your ability. Confidence is a result of practice. Say that you spend an hour on the practice tee, hitting 8-iron shots. With each good shot you increase your confidence, and when you transport that confidence to the course, you'll hit the same successful shots in competition.

When you stop and think about it, bogey golf in club competition is pretty darn good. One way to insure a bogey is to stay out of serious trouble. If you do get into trouble, get out as quickly and directly as you can. At a golf school last summer in Minneapolis, Jim Flick was preparing to give his group a three-hole playing lesson. The group was about to tee off on a par-5 hole when Flick called three women aside.

"What do you expect to shoot on this hole?" he asked. "You'll certainly settle for a six, won't you? A seven wouldn't be too bad, either, would it?" The women relaxed, secure in the knowledge that Flick did not expect them to hit three perfect shots.

A realistic mental approach to golf is essential in the mixed tournaments that have become so popular recently. It's become an "in" thing to play golf with your husband on Sunday afternoons. I'm all for that type of competition, but I can sympathize with the man whose wife attempts to pull off an impossible shot and knocks it into the water. What a strain that can sometimes place on the round and the marriage.

Instruction, practice and a knowledge of the limits of your game can make those mixed tournaments a lot more fun. It also helps, of course, to have a partner who has a relaxed and tolerant attitude. I can't think of a more pleasant way to spend a lazy summer afternoon.

The format I like is an alternate shot form of competition with selected drives. The husband and wife each drive, then choose the tee shot that sets up the best strategical way to score. The most ideal sequence on a par-4 hole is to use the woman's drive, if possible, and have the man hit the iron shot to the green. Men have the strength to hit down into the ball more firmly with the irons, promoting greater backspin.

That was the formula most of us tried to employ in the Pepsi-Cola Mixed Team Championship that was won by Chi Chi Rodriguez and Joann Washam in December, 1976, at Doral. Joann is one of the best drivers on the women's tour and Chi Chi is a superb short-iron player. My partner was Tom Nieporte and, although we were never in contention, we had fun. It was the first renewal of mixed team golf for the professionals in 10 years, and I hope it becomes a fixture.

Remember, golf can be every bit as enjoyable for women as it is for men. Club golf, unlike the golf we play on the tour, is merely a game. It's an outlet for fun and a chance to compete in beautiful surroundings. Give it your best, but always with the realization that your happiness and your livelihood are not riding on the next shot.

10.

NEW COMPETITIVE CHALLENGES

Billie Jean King and I were having a friendly debate one day a few years ago at the Boca Raton Hotel in Florida about which sport is the most difficult to play well. I thought it was golf and, of course, Billie Jean was holding out for tennis.

She knew I had played baseball in grammar school and basketball and tennis at Rollins. "If you were to classify your skill in tennis, using handicaps the way you do in golf," she asked, "what handicap would you give yourself in tennis?"

I replied it would probably be an eight, which would be equivalent to about an 80 shooter in golf.

Billie Jean thought about that for a few moments. Finally I asked her what she shot in golf.

"I don't know," she said. "I've never played enough golf to find out."

Since we were both curious, I got her some clubs from the pro shop and we went right out and played the Boca Raton course. Or tried to. It took us more than two hours to get in the first five holes.

Billie Jean King, with her super eye-hand coordination, had found a sport that had her licked. She set up wrong over the ball because she had no idea of the right way, and she could not keep the ball in play. Her score that day was 120.

"In case anybody ever asks you," I laughed, "your golf handicap is about 40. Now what were you saying about the toughest sport to learn?"

Actually, there is a marked similarity between the swings in golf and in tennis. The pivot, the move into the left side, the leg action and the fluid motion of the stroke all are essential to both sports. Several athletes I know play them both with great skill. Althea Gibson, for one; Wendy Overton, my old Rollins roommate, has a 12 handicap in golf. I consider myself a reasonably good tennis player, and I understand Jack Nicklaus plays a fast game.

Not long after that experience with Billie Jean, I discovered golf was a cakewalk compared to some other sports. I learned it the hard way, in the Women's Superstars.

This competition came about as the result of a little agitation from a group of women, Billie Jean and I among them. We were griping, as usual, about the inequality in sports between men and women. The men already had their TV Superstars event. Why not one for the women?

Remind me never to take you rowing. This event in the Women's Superstars nearly left me upstream without a paddle.

Larry King helped set it up for us. Sandra Palmer, who had been a good basketball player in high school, and I represented the LPGA in the preliminary eliminations, held in December of 1974 at the Houston Astrodome. There were 10 events, including bowling, swimming, running the hurdles, throwing a softball, basketball free throws and the 440-yard dash. We could enter seven events.

The 440-yard run just about killed me, but the thing I remember most about the Superstars competition was when the attorney for Robin Smith, the jockey, claimed I had stepped over the line in the softball throw. As a result, I had to forfeit one throw and finished seventh. I did not qualify for the finals two months later at Rotunda, Fla.

As things turned out, it wouldn't have made much difference if I had qualified. A few weeks later, when Billie Jean was a guest in my home at Highland Beach, she was trying to teach me a dance step to the recording of Elton John's "Saturday Night." I tripped on the carpet-

The competition was fierce at Rotunda. Anne Henning (right), beats Karen Logan (left) and Irene Shea to the tape.

ing and tore ligaments in my left ankle. Beautiful. And the opening of the 1975 tour season was just around the corner.

I had the cast removed from my left leg on the Wednesday before the Burdine's tournament in Miami. What a sight. One leg was brown from the Florida sun and the other was milky white. I rode around in a cart while playing in the pro-am and had to soak my foot in a bucket of ice for the rest of the week.

Well, wouldn't you know it, I led the tournament after 36 holes. I didn't play all that well the last day and finished third, but it wasn't a bad performance for a cripple. One reason for my good play, as I look back on it, was that I didn't want to take any chances by swinging too hard. On nearly every shot I used more club than I normally would, and I compensated by swinging easier. It's something all of us should remember. I knew I had plenty of club, so I just swung it with less effort and it paid off.

Getting back to the Superstars, I was anxious to compete the following year for several reasons. First, I had been instrumental in its origin, but then had failed to qualify for the finals. Second, I wanted to prove my athletic ability against what I knew would be a really strong field. Finally, there was the chance to make some big money—as Anne Henning was to prove when she earned $51,400 for finishing in first place that year.

The Women's Superstars of 1976, held again at Rotunda, was a milestone in women's sports. It afforded a real opportunity for those who excelled in areas in which they had not previously been able to capitalize financially, such as speed skating, diving and track. It brought 24 women athletes together for three days of intensive competition before a national television audience. Friendships were cemented, and so were a few business deals.

It was really a heyday for the women who had no professional outlets for their skills. This was their big chance, and they prepared for it accordingly. I learned that Micki King, the diver, had trained for six months by running two miles a day in combat boots. More than anything else, it was a pro Olympics. The Superstars had been originally intended as a challenge of hand and eye coordination, but it developed instead into a test of strength.

What a field of female athletes were there! Anne Henning, Jean Balukas, Laura Blears Ching, Linda Jefferson, Micki King, Karen Logan, Annedore Richter, Kiki Cutter, Althea Gibson and Irene Shea finished in places one through 10. Martina Navratilova and Wyomia Tyus, two women I thought would contend, were a distant 11th and 12th. The golfing contingent of Amy Alcott, Joann Washam and myself were far back in the pack.

Also on hand were swimmers Diana Nyad and Keena Rothhammer; Shirley (Cha-Cha) Muldowney, a drag racer; Monique Proulx, a blonde auto racer who formerly taught French and did fashion modeling; and Jackie Tonawanda, a 165-pound New York boxer.

The competition was rough, with several casualties. Keena Rothhammer, the swimmer, got racked up in the obstacle course and had to be rushed to a hospital near Rotunda. Joann Washam chipped her ankle in the same event, an injury that had to be a factor in her disappointing year on tour in 1976. Althea Gibson, Irene Shea, Laura Blears Ching and skier Genia Fuller suffered pulled muscles. It was a miracle that Laura, banged up as she was in the finals, managed to finish third.

The Superstars changed my outlook on Olympic-style competition for women. I found out I had little taste for this hard-nosed, bruising combat. These sports were not only tougher than golf, they weren't nearly as much fun. I emerged from those three days with a greater appreciation than ever of my own sport.

Something else came out of the Superstars: the Women's Professional Softball League, in which I was soon deeply—and happily—involved.

Karen Logan's sport is basketball, but look at her skim the hurdles!

That was where I first met Joan Joyce. Joan had been the star pitcher for the Raybestos Brakettes, the world champions of women's softball. Billie Jean and I had a long talk with her one evening. We learned that she had pitched over 150 no-hitters and 60 perfect games, and yet what real recognition had she received? My name was in the newspapers and on television frequently for golf, and so was Billie Jean's for tennis, but Joan was far superior in her field than I was in mine. Something was obviously wrong.

Billie Jean, Joan and I were sitting around over chocolate sundaes one night—this was during the preliminaries for the first Superstars, in December, 1974, at Houston—talking about women's sports. Billie Jean started asking Joan questions about softball. Apparently, she thought it was then a professional sport.

"Why aren't you playing professionally?" Billie Jean asked. "Why play for only a few months during the summer? Why are you an amateur . . . and why don't you do something about it?"

Joan told her that the world tournament at Stratford, Conn., had drawn more than 150,000 people in one week, which prompted Billie Jean to think that the sponsors had made a lot of money. Then Joan went on, not making a pitch or anything, but just stating facts: more people played softball than any other sport, people from every walk of life.

We decided it would be fun to channel all this talent and interest into a professional league. Then we left it there and went our own ways. It seems in this life that a lot of people have ideas, but very few follow up on them. Joan's last comment was, "It sounds great, but who'd put up the money? And who'd take the time and energy to get it started?"

Later that winter we met in Boston to watch a Virginia Slims tennis circuit match. By this time Joan had some additional facts and figures about the potential of professional softball, and we were more enthusiastic than ever.

"Billie Jean and I are going to own a team in this league," I said, "and you, Joan Joyce, are going to be our pitcher." Then we started giggling about it, and how much fun it would be to sit in the stands, eating popcorn, watching our own team play.

One fortunate thing about Billie Jean, aside from her ability, exposure and tremendous energy, is that she has some people behind her who can put ideas into reality. Her husband Larry for one. Larry made some calls which caused Denis Murphy to enter the picture. Denis Murphy must be one of the great organizers in the history of pro sports. He was in on the establishment of the American Basketball Association, the World Hockey Association and World Team Tennis. None of them bombed out.

After talking to us, Denis immediately sounded out 40 potential sponsors for the softball venture and came up with 10. As a result, we were able to start league competition in 1976. The divisional setup and the charter team members went like this: Western Division—Santa Ana

Race driver Monique Proulx struggles in the free throw contest.

Lionettes, San Jose Sunbirds, San Diego Sandpipers, Phoenix Phoenixbirds and Southern California Gems (based in San Bernardino); Eastern Division—Connecticut Falcons, Michigan Travelers, Chicago Ravens, Pennsylvania Liberties and Buffalo Breskies.

We called our league "the first real vehicle of opportunity for women in professional team sport." And it was. "We don't have to worry about the women being exploited," Billie Jean said. "The owners will sign up the players who can win. Winning is the important thing."

All of the women who signed had to turn professional. When you think pro sports, you think of those whopping salaries in football, basketball, baseball and hockey. Well, this was a little different. Each girl was paid between $1,000 and $4,000 for the season. That's not much in comparison to other sports, but before we came along it was costing *them* money to play amateur softball. We tried to keep the salaries under $50,000 per team, so none of the teams would fold the first year. None of them did.

We had learned that softball was a game of the middle class and we didn't want to take this league away from them. Ticket prices were therefore reasonable. For example, in our park at Meriden the admission price was $2.50. Heck, you can't even get into a movie for that these days. We set a 120-game schedule for each team, with most of the games doubleheaders. That meant at least 2½ hours of entertainment each night. To minimize traveling costs, each of the Coast teams made only one trip to the other Coast. We flew on that trip, and all season the players stayed in good motels.

Joan, who had played her amateur softball in Stratford, convinced us to base our team in Meriden, more accessible to the greater population areas of Connecticut. Abe Grossman, the mayor of Meriden, fell in love with the Connecticut Falcons. He attended nearly every home game at Falcon Field, which he had built for us in only 28 days. It was created out of the woods, with bleachers and lights and a parking area. Abe Grossman is proud of Falcon Field, and all of us are just as proud of him.

Our team budget for the season was $220,000. We raised about $75,000 in subscriptions and contributions. I put in $10,000 of my own money. We averaged $1,500 for our home dates, and wound up the season losing about $30,000, which wasn't bad for a first-year venture.

One of our fund-raising events was a celebrity day in early June involving 20 of the tour golfers who came up to Meriden after we had finished the Girl Talk Classic in New Rochelle, N.Y. They played an 18-hole pro-am during the day and a softball game that night. That was some show. Carol Mann, tall and impressive, umpired. She dusted off home plate with a full-sized broom. Playing against the Falcons, with Joan pitching for our team, were some real characters: Bonnie Bryant on third base, Pam Higgins on second, Betty Burfeindt on first. I played shortstop. Sandra Haynie was a demon center fielder, flanked by Joann Washam, Jan Ferraris and Penny Pulz.

Here I am taking a whack at bat in our 1976 fund-raising softall game for the Falcons that many of the women golf pros played in.

I don't know who got the biggest kick out of that game, the Falcons or the tour golfers, but we all enjoyed it. So did the fans. I was particularly happy to play against those talented Falcons, because as a girl growing up I thought I wanted to be a great ballplayer. I used to idolize Joe DiMaggio and Mickey Mantle. My heroes were, in fact, all male athletes.

That night I looked around the stands and saw so many kids there that I wondered to myself, "If this women's softball thing makes it, the young girls who are watching us will have some real women athletes to look up to. They can grow up to be another Joan Joyce or Irene Shea. And by the time they do, they'll be making some real money at it—maybe $20,000 a year or more. Softball won't be a sideline for the women, it will be a full-time job. We'll have drafts and scouts, just like a real major league club."

That's the real beauty of pro softball for women. While it was true that Billie Jean and I went into this venture partly as an ego thing, because we were frustrated team jocks, this was also my first real chance to give something back to women's sports. I've made nearly $400,000 playing golf, but an athlete like Joan Joyce never had that opportunity. Maybe the Joan Joyces of the future will.

I truly think Joan is the Babe Zaharias of her time. Not only is she the greatest female softball pitcher who ever lived, she is also a fine golfer. Her goal is to eventually win a player's card at the LPGA qualifying school and join our tour.

That will be a double challenge, for Joan and for our softball team, but isn't that what life is all about? I've been enjoying the spirit of challenge ever since I can remember, and when my golf days are over I can begin to channel my competitive instincts into maintaining our winning tradition in softball.

Did I say winning? You bet. The Connecticut Falcons finished on top of our division in 1976 and went on to sweep the playoffs in seven straight games for the world championship. Just like the Cincinnati Reds. We were lucky enough to hit the jackpot in our first year.

I'm glad Joan, Billie Jean and I had that little talk at the Superstars.

Joan Joyce, who has to be the greatest female softball pitcher ever, serves up her no-hitters for the Connecticut Falcons.

11.
THE FUTURE OF WOMEN'S SPORTS

While visiting with my parents in New Hampshire recently, I picked up the Boston Globe and noticed on the front page a picture of some women playing rugby. In the accompanying article, one of the women was asked why she played such a strenuous sport. "Because it's a great release," she replied. "It's so exhilarating to compete."

How right she is. I often think of it that way—the exhilaration of competition. It is one of the keys to happiness and success for all of us. Competition is not always related to sports, either. In life, you must compete to be successful. High school students compete for better grades and acceptance into college. College students compete for the best job offers. Executives compete in business situations. Lawyers compete in the courtroom. The horizons are just beginning to widen for women. Society is finally opening the doors.

As far as I'm concerned, competition among women is the best thing that ever happened to our society, and it has helped to enrich the lives of all of us. Things were different when I was growing up. It wasn't considered "cricket" for women to compete. Girls who took part in sports were considered tomboys. In high school, if a guy took you out on a tennis date, it was bad form to beat him because he probably would never ask you out again.

The truth is that men were taught for a long time to condition their bodies while women were encouraged to pamper theirs. Now, more and more, we women are conditioning and toning our bodies to the fullest. We've learned that the better your body works, the sharper your brain functions. These days you can see women lifting weights to develop muscles. What's wrong with that? I can't imagine a man wanting a puny woman when he can have someone who is firm and solid. I've read where women athletes make the best lovers, and I think that's true.

In my area around Boca Raton, nearly every divorced man who has remarried has chosen a younger woman—someone with whom he can share the fun and activity of sports. These marriages have a "buddy" quality. The woman becomes not only a wife, but a partner on the golf course or tennis court as well. Most men want more than a woman who is busy with her bridge club, her garden group or simply involved in cleaning the house. I'd like to know who started this woman-belongs-in-the-house business, anyway.

Exquisite form is exhibited by Olga Korbut in Moscow, 1973.

People occasionally ask me if I'd ever marry a professional athlete. I don't think so. It would be like a double marriage. I'm married to golf now, and the male professional athlete is married to his sport. The demands on our time and emotions would be too severe. The women's golf tour is virtually a year-round operation.

If I decided on it, though, I could bring one major advantage to this type of marriage. I would be able to understand my husband's pressures and moods. The professional who comes home after losing a big game is enduring an agony that only those of us who have experienced it could ever comprehend. But for the present, I'll stick to golf.

Women are proud of the fact that it is now an "in" thing to be an athlete and proud of the evoluton of women in sports. The progress made by women in golf and tennis is phenomenal—and just beginning. The overall growth is so astounding that I predict women will be participating in contact sports such as football within the next 20 years—something that was unthinkable only a short time ago. Women are already playing hockey and flag football, a more physical variation of touchball. (To stop the ball carrier, you pull the flag out of her pocket). You think there's no contact in this game? Ask the women who come home with bruised shoulders and knees. They love it.

The Olympics have shown what women can accomplish in gymnastics, ice skating, track, volleyball and swimming. The names of Olga Korbut, Nadia Comaneci, Sheila Young, Dorothy Hamill and Micki King have become as familiar to sports fans as their male counterparts. These champions, moreover, have inspired thousands of young girls to enter competition at all levels and in all sports—many of which were once considered the male domain.

Professional tennis, for example, now offers fantastic financial opportunities for good players such as Chris Evert and Evonne Goolagong, who have made fortunes on and off the court. Eventually, our softball league will become as lucrative for the team-sport female athlete. Joan Joyce is now the highest paid member of the professional staff at Uniroyal, whose equipment she endorses.

I also foresee a tremendous increase among women as spectators at sporting events. It looked as if at least half the people at the 1977 Super Bowl were women. They attend professional football games not only because it's something to share with their husbands, but because they like and understand the sport. When I first joined the tour, men composed the majority of our galleries. Now women make up about 50 percent.

And not only are more women watching golf tournaments, more are buying equipment and playing the game.

One reason why golf is so popular with women is that it is one of the few sports in which you can compete and socialize at the same time. I don't mean a tour event, because we're all business out there, but in club tournaments or a simple Sunday round. On the course

Skating champion Dorothy Hamill cuts a neat figure.

146

there's no net separating you from your opponent. You can walk along and talk about politics, gossip about last night's party or plan next month's charity drive. Nice, normal conversation. The golf course has been the venue of many business deals and the catalyst for many a love affair.

Because women lack the strength of men, we used to be relegated in the male mind to the status of powderpuff hitters. That's not true anymore. New concepts of golf instruction, featuring fuller arm motion and a more emphatic transfer of weight from the right to the left side in the downswing, have provided the dimension and the enjoyment of added distance for women players. Babe Zaharias was once considered a freak because she could drive the ball 250 yards; but lately I have seen several talented young amateurs, such as Nancy Lopez, do it consistently.

Women will continue to improve their distance and the overall quality of their games with more competition. A woman club champion can expect to be challenged the next year by half a dozen hopeful rivals, each confident that her game will be sharpened by the previous year's tournament play. Competition brings out the best in us and inspires us to improve.

I don't have to tell you what a wonderful family sport golf is. All over the country I see married couples playing in foursomes with their children. Could anything bring a family closer together? Many times you'll see the husband playing with his associates, and the wife with hers. Children have playing privileges at most clubs. Afterward the family members get back together and the stories fly. "Oh, you should have seen the slice I made on the fifth hole today," or "I hit my best drive of the season on No. 7."

Golf's broad appeal for players of all levels results from the handicapping system. It's the great equalizer, enabling golfers of various skill levels to compete with a fair opportunity to win. I don't know of any one element of the game that does more to create a wholesome, legitimate competitive atmosphere.

Unlike tennis, in which the competitive aspect is obvious, in golf it is more subtle. Golf's basic competition is the player against the course. Occasionally, in a group of two, three or four players, it requires the stimulation of an additional element, a pot at the end of the rainbow. If this sounds as though I am suggesting some form of wagering on the course, I am. It's a stimulating way of creating your own competition.

I'm very much against those $500 nassaus I know some men play at their clubs. They can get just as much enjoyment out of a round with $1 on each nine. With handicap adjustment, a man can play his wife, son or daughter for 10 cents a hole, like my dad and I used to do.

It's amazing what golf has done for my life. When I was teaching school back in Portsmouth, I used to sit in the classroom and occasionally

Chris Evert, the highest-paid female tennis player in the world.

My friend Sally Little, a charmer who turns tiger on the golf course.

browse through magazines and travel books, dreaming of trips to Bermuda or Europe. Since then golf has taken me to Japan five times, London four times, Australia twice. I've played in Ireland, Switzerland, Sweden, the Philippines and Hong Kong.

Anyone can visit these countries as a tourist, but as a golfer I've competed with people from foreign lands and gotten to know them as they really are. We dine in the best restaurants, not the tourist traps. In Mexico I participated in fiestas, and I watched bullfights staged especially for the tour players.

Through my friendships with Wendy Overton and Billie Jean King, I've seen Wimbledon from the inside—visited the locker room, chatted with Chris Evert before a big match, met Jimmy Connors and Ilie Nastase.

Golf has also given me the opportunity to participate in pro-ams and celebrity outings. I've been paired several times in pro-ams with

Joe DiMaggio. What a great guy. He was one of the finest baseball players who ever lived, but he's never become an outstanding golfer. Joe is happy to shoot 80 any time he plays. Earlier I talked about my experiences with Bobby Orr. Some other of my pro-am partners have included Jerry West, Jerry Lucas, Fred Biletnikoff and George Blanda.

I was the first woman to compete in the Dewar's Celebrity Tennis Tournament at the Riviera Hotel in Las Vegas, a two-day event involving 16 professional athletes. One year I took part in a celebrity pro-am golf tournament in Nashville, and Sandra Palmer and I were the first women to be invited. Minneapolis has a big charity tournament each year and it used to be a stag affair, but Marlene Hagge and Mary Cushing have been celebrity guests the last two years.

Although I am fortunate in having been a beneficiary of the increased interest in women athletes, the real significance is that things are looking up for all women—and not just in Las Vegas, Nashville and Minneapolis. While world travel, mingling with celebrities and earning $150,000 a year make up a lifestyle that most women can only dream about, it is a lifestyle that is becoming a reality for more and more women each year.

Evidence of this can be found in television's increased awareness of the woman's role in sports, particularly in the CBS series called the "Challenge of the Sexes." The golf competition, consisting of nine-hole matches, is filmed at Mission Viejo in California. They give the women an advantage of about 30 yards on the tees. In 1975 I shot 37 and lost by a stroke to Hale Irwin. Laura Baugh beat Doug Sanders the next year, and in 1977 Jan Stephenson beat Raymond Floyd. Jan picked up $5,000 for that little day's work.

In the near future you'll see a greater involvement of women players in golf apparel. This market hasn't even begun to be tapped. Laura Baugh was the first to have her own line of golf clothes and she's done very well with it. Manufacturers, content for years merely to create apparel endorsed by men, are just starting to capitalize on the exposure that women golfers are receiving.

Women are not only endorsing this quality apparel, the more attractive ones are modeling it. They are also appearing in television commercials, promoting many different types of products. Laura Baugh won a Clio award a few years ago for the Ultra-Brite "Love Life" commercial. Jan Stephenson and Sally Little, with their charm and beauty, ought to be perfect for television promotion.

One reason for the general upsurge of interest in women's golf is that men can better relate to our technique and our games than to the male pros. We hit the ball about the same distance as a competent male amateur, and we face the same problems on the course. Men enjoy watching women play golf, because of the similarity in skill levels. They can learn something by observing us.

I can think of no better example than David Foster, chairman of the

Colgate-Palmolive Company. David is an absolute golf nut. He's probably the most successful businessman you can find anywhere, but his fondest wish is to be a great golfer. He's pretty darn good now, a 6-handicapper and a very tough competitor. But the closest he can get to high level competitive golf is to sponsor tournaments, which enables him to play with us in practice and pro-am rounds.

Colgate's involvement with the LPGA has been an enormous boost to the upgrading of women's golf, but in a way it has also held us back. In the process of spending millions of dollars on women's golf, Colgate has become the dominant commercial influence. The prospect of settling for No. 2 has turned away many other potential corporate sponsors. We lost Sears and Sealy because of this situation.

Thanks to the efforts of our commissioner, Ray Volpe, and his marketing specialist, Tony Andrea, several other major firms are becoming associated with the LPGA tour. The Northwestern Mutual Life Insurance Company is one. In 1976 it inaugurated the Women's International, a quality tournament in every way, at Moss Creek on Hilton Head Island. We knew things would be first class when we discovered every ball on the practice tee was brand new.

What an asset Ray Volpe has been to the LPGA. In future years we'll look back upon his appointment as commissioner in 1975 as the turning point in our success. Volpe's greatest contribution, aside from his role in the elevation of purses, has been to generate an awareness of the tour among the general public. "The LPGA has always had a good product," he once told me, "but it needs marketing. We must let the sponsors and the galleries know what we have to offer."

The future of professional women's golf is bright and glistening. Not too far down the road we'll be playing all our tournaments with a $100,000 minimum in prize money. The old tournaments that offered $45,000 purses and made a lot of money, like the Portland Classic, will have to keep in step or they'll be replaced.

We'll have more tournaments each year on television with better quality telecasts. The most articulate women players will serve as TV commentators, offering an insight into our games that has all too often been lacking.

I was discussing these subjects on a flight one day with Frank Chirkinian, the CBS producer who does such outstanding work each year at the Masters and other CBS tournaments. Frank is very much interested in women's golf. He said that women are in about the same place the men were 15 years ago, before the big increase in their purses. He is right. A few years ago the women were playing for about an eighth of what the men were playing for. Now it's about a third. The men have virtually reached a plateau in prize money, but the women's tour is growing sharply each year. The big money is just starting to come.

In order to perpetuate our tour on a high-quality basis, we need a constant flow of fresh playing talent. In the past that has been a prob-

Japan's Chako Higuchi likes the big-money purses over here.

Silvia Bertolaccini, Argentina's contribution to the women's tour.

lem. The good young amateurs did not always pursue a career in professional golf, simply because it was not the thing to do. They could make more money working at a job, while playing golf as a hobby. Barb McIntire and Judy Bell are two examples. They run a successful apparel shop at the Broadmoor Hotel in Colorado Springs, Colo., competing in the big women's amateur events. It wasn't worth it for them 20 years ago to join the tour. But it is for the young women of today.

The recent increase in purses, the growing exposure on television and the general stature of women's professional golf have attracted a wave of young talent like Amy Alcott, Hollis Stacy, Laura Baugh, Pat Bradley, Mary Bea Porter and Debbie Massey. Our LPGA qualifying schools will continue to supply promising rookies each year. They'll come from summer instructional clinics at municipal courses and country clubs, from high school golf teams and the colleges. Tulsa University is offering women's golf scholarships in an active program administered by Dale McNamara, who is an excellent golfer herself.

In the 1977 Bing Crosby tournament, Nancy Lopez of Tulsa and Marianne Bretton of UCLA were participants. Their handicaps were each adjusted by six strokes, but they hit from the men's tees. And the galleries loved them.

Foreign-born players are pouring over to capitalize on the financial opportunities of the tour, and in years to come the invasion will multiply. Chako Higuchi of Japan, Silvia Bertolaccini of Argentina, Jan Stephenson and Penny Pulz of Australia and Sally Little of South Africa are all talented players who add a great deal of flavor to the tour, not only in ability but in personality and gallery appeal. Jan won two tournaments in 1976, and Sally holed a shot out of a sand trap to win one.

For the last two years the low scorer in our LPGA Winter Qualifying School has come from Taiwan. Tu-Ai-Yu was the medalist in 1976 and went on to play quite well on the tour that year. In 1977 the leader was Eva Chang, a 27-year-old veteran of the Japanese LPGA tour. Eva outshot a strong field in cold weather to earn her card, then tied for ninth in the opening LPGA event of the year at Miami. We'll be hearing a lot more from her.

The next great source of talent could be Great Britain. The British Isles have been way behind the times; the women over there have hardly any rights at all, at least where golf is concerned. It's difficult for them to get on courses and they have few tournaments to enter. I like what I've seen of Michelle Walker, an English girl, and there'll be others.

The caliber of women's golf in Japan is improving all the time. Chako was the breakthrough. Now the Japanese are inviting us over to their tournaments and they're studying our swings and our techniques, the way the Japanese do. Soon we'll have a lot of Chakos over here.

Reflecting on the way things were 10 years ago and looking ahead to what's over the next hill, I get a feeling of tremendous exhilaration. The next generation is going to have it so much better. If I have had any part in that, it's all been worthwhile. It has been richly satisfying for me to be involved in the women's tour as it has grown and prospered, and to have helped create the opportunities for players of the future.

CAREER RECORD

VICTORIES

1970
Lady Carling Open

1971
George Washington Classic
Lady Pepsi Classic

1972
Colgate- Dinah Shore Winners Circle
Suzuki Golf Internationale
Angelo's Four-Ball Championship (with Sandra Palmer)
Dallas Civitan Open
Lady Errol Classic

1973
Angelo's Four-Ball Championship (with Sandra Palmer)

1974
Birmingham Classic
Southgate Open
Lady Errol Classic
Bing Crosby Guadalajara

1975
Karsten Ping Classic
Colgate Triple Crown
World Ladies Classic

1976
Wheeling Classic
Dallas Civitan Open
World Ladies Classic

1977
Colgate Triple Crown

MAJOR AWARDS

1969
Rookie of Year

1970
LPGA/Golf Digest Most Improved Golfer

1971
LPGA/Golf Digest Most Improved Golfer

CAREER EARNINGS

YEAR	MONEY WINNINGS	RANK	STROKE AVERAGE
1969	$ 3,825	37	76.84
1970	12,060	13	74.76
1971	34,493	3	73.22
1972	57,323	2	73.41
1973	40,711	9	73.59
1974	86,422	2	73.11
1975	45,478	6	73.00
1976	93,616	4	72.52

Total money winnings through Jan. 1, 1977: $373,929.

PHOTOGRAPH CREDITS:

Julius Baum, p. 10
Bailey Campbell Advertising, p. 125
Joan Chandler, pp. 59, 134, 135, 137, 138, 143
Courier-Journal & Louisville Times, p. 122
Dunlop Sports Enterprises, p. 44
Albert Evans, courtesy R & A Photofeatures, Ltd., p. 148
Robert Galvin, p. 80
Frank Gardner, pp. 56, 67
David Gruber, pp. 116, 118, 129
Will Hertzberg, pp. 52, 153
Harry Holstine, pp. 109, 156
Milton Jones, p. 73
E. D. Lacey, p. 53
Ladies' Professional Golf Association, pp. 73, 154
Manchester Union Leader, p. 31
Tom Mathews, courtesy Birmingham (Ala.) News, p. 62
John P. May, p. 61
Bill Mount, pp. 14, 15, 48, 85, 86, 92, 102, 114
Lester Nehamkin, pp. 72, 80, 132
John Newcomb, p. 105
Portsmouth Herald, pp. 24, 26
Jack Scagnetti, pp. 64, 150
Peter Travers, pp. 58, 60
United Press International, pp. 72, 76-77, 144, 147
Gerald Viegen, p. 19
Bob Walsh, courtesy St. Paul Pioneer Press, p. 68
Frank White, pp. 32, 41, 98, 141